Powerful
Public
Relations

A How-To Guide for Libraries

RASHELLE S. KARP, Editor

FOR THE
Library Administration and
Management Association

AMERICAN LIBRARY ASSOCIATION
Chicago and London
2002

While extensive effort has gone into ensuring the reliability of information appearing in this book, the publisher makes no warranty, express or implied, on the accuracy or reliability of the information, and does not assume and hereby disclaims any liability to any person for any loss or damage caused by errors or omissions in this publication.

Cover and text design by Dianne M. Rooney

Composition by ALA Editions in Bodoni and Franklin Gothic using QuarkXPress 4.1 on a PC platform

Printed on 50-pound white offset, a pH-neutral stock, and bound in 10-point cover stock by Data Reproductions

The paper used in this publication meets the minimum requirements of American National Standard for Information Sciences—Permanence of Paper for Printed Library Materials, ANSI Z39.48-1992. ∞

Library of Congress Cataloging-in-Publication Data

Powerful public relations : a how-to guide for libraries /
    Rashelle S. Karp, editor.
        p.   cm.
    "For the Library Administration and Management
Association."
    Includes bibliographical references and index.
    ISBN 0-8389-0818-7 (alk. paper)
    1. Libraries—Public relations—United States.   I. Karp,
Rashelle S.   II. Library Administration and Management
Association.

Z716.3 .P69 2002
021.7′0973–dc21

                                                    2001053281

Printed in the United States of America

06 05 04 03 02   5 4 3 2 1

CONTENTS

FIGURES

INTRODUCTION

WILLIAM BUCHANAN

Since the first edition of this book appeared, the day-to-day lives of librarians—indeed, of virtually all citizens in technologically developed countries—have been dramatically altered by the rapid and continuing evolution of the World Wide Web and its associated technologies. The notion of the library as a revered institution supported by loyal and dependable patrons is being gradually supplanted by the notion that the library is one of many information and knowledge institutions competing for customers. Consequently, the role of marketing and public relations for the library in the 21st century is increasingly important as librarians seek new and more innovative ways to make their institutions relevant, competitive, and visible in the information marketplace.

The updated edition of this information-rich volume provides working librarians with easily understood chapters that address both the why and how of public relations. It incorporates and expands upon the text of the original book, which addressed traditional approaches to public relations through the development of programs, displays, library publications, and good relations with the news media. Then—as now—the purpose of good public relations is seen as the development of ongoing programs of contact between librarians and the population groups they serve. Since the original volume appeared, librarians' abilities to develop these ongoing programs of contact have been supercharged by the World Wide Web and related technologies. In chapters new to this volume, Chandler Jackson ("Web-Based Public Relations") and Susan Hilton ("Interactive Multimedia Programs via Touch Screen Kiosks and CD-ROMs") examine and give examples of the roles of these new technologies in library public relations programs. These chapters, combined with the updated chapters from the previous edition, result in an easy-to-use volume rich in both theory and practical suggestions.

Though much has changed in the world of communications since the first edition of this book appeared, much has remained the same. In the introduction to the first edition I wrote that "For many, the phrase 'public relations' conjures up images of Madison Avenue executives who polish and promote a product beyond recognition. The modus operandi of such executives is the 'blitz campaign,' in which the product is showcased in a star-studded series of high-profile publicity 'splashes.'

"This is *not* the stuff of which library public relations campaigns are made. To be sure, librarians can, should, and, in fact, do develop programming around special events that are highly publicized. But the purpose of a library's public relations program is not the quick-sell, publicity-at-any-price mentality.

"The purpose of library public relations is to develop ongoing programs of contact between the librarians and the population groups that they serve."[1] This view of library public relations is still a valid one. We are not spin doctors and we are not trying to convince a gullible public to buy something they neither want nor need. We are service-oriented professionals trying to make our institutions as user-friendly and user-oriented as we can. Public relations is a tool to help us accomplish this important task. This book can greatly enhance the ability of a librarian to effectively and efficiently add one more item to his or her list of job duties. Even so, the public relations part of a librarian's job is not accomplished without the investment of time and planning energy. Why should you make this investment? Is the investment going to be a worthwhile one for your library?

The answers to these questions now are essentially the same as they were five years ago when the first edition of this book appeared: "The answer to these questions is, in part, in the definition of the institution itself: libraries are institutions designed for use. In order to be used, libraries must be familiar to user groups. A public relations program allows the library staff to maintain positive, supportive communications with the library's public, including current and potential users. A public relations program provides a systematic, ongoing means by which library staff can communicate with, report to, and receive feedback from active and potential user groups.

"As libraries change, evolve, and expand their services, they continuously develop the potential for attracting new clientele and providing more and better services for existing clientele. This potential is most likely to be fully realized when the clientele that can benefit from the library's services is kept informed about what is available."[2]

In 1995 I pointed to the appearance of video collections in libraries as a dramatic example of how new services and publicity of those services positively impact both the library and its service community. In the past five years we have seen this dramatic example eclipsed by the decision of many libraries to offer public access computing and Internet services. The availability of ports on the World Wide Web at the library—be it public, school, or academic—has brought increased patron flow into libraries. Many libraries took the opportunity of the announcement of these new services to promote the library as the "place to be." And new generations of library users have discovered that, indeed, the library is the "place to be."

As the authors of the chapters in this book demonstrate, library public relations can be achieved in many ways, including newsletters and other library publications, press releases, public services announcements, displays, exhibits, and special programming. These are activities that can and should involve more than just the library director—librarians, library staff, and library volunteers can all participate. This book is, in fact, aimed at all these levels of potential participants in a library public relations program.

The relatively small size of this book is actually a metaphor for one of its most important messages: brevity. Good public relations does not waste the consumer's time with unnecessary words and images. It gets to the point quickly and imaginatively, just like this book does. In its pages you will find both theoretical and how-to chapters written by specialists whose aim is to provide straightforward, no-nonsense advice for developing effective public relations programs for libraries. With this book in hand, librarians have the necessary information to develop public relations campaigns that will make their institutions competitive, relevant, and highly visible in the information marketplace.

NOTES

1. William Buchanan, introduction to *Part-Time Public Relations with Full-Time Results,* ed. Rashelle S. Karp (Chicago: American Library Association, 1995), ix.

2. Ibid.

Synergy in Library Public Relations, Marketing, and Development Activities

KATHARINA J. BLACKSTEAD AND ERIC C. SHOAF

Proactive library public relations begins with the design of marketing and development activities that work together as they communicate a central theme. Today's busy library professionals need to "work smart" by creating a basic concept once and then using it for many different purposes. Fortunately, the many elements of library public relations can emanate from a common information base, with customized enhancements for each aspect providing functional distinctions between them. Keeping this in mind can save a great deal of time and effort.

LIBRARY PUBLIC RELATIONS

All library publicity efforts should have a common core of information that is constantly "refreshed" in reaction to changing library environments. Some examples of information in this core include the mission of the library, size of library holdings and other statistical measures, budget information, user demographics, collections of note, grants and awards, specialized services, and new acquisitions. These facts and figures should be presented within the context of engaging descriptive rhetoric wherever possible.

The common core of information is often publicized in the form of:

- press releases
- informational flyers of all types
- open position advertisements
- new appointment and retirement announcements
- media advertisements
- articles
- program announcements

Longer publications are another good tool for presenting a library's common core of information. These can include:

- internal and external newsletters
- catalogs
- books
- brochures and library guides
- articles by library staff
- electronic publications

Exhibits of library materials, developed through the subject and technical expertise of library staff or external contributors, can be recycled into some of the publicity vehicles mentioned above. Ever-widening use of the World Wide Web makes it an excellent tool for all advancement activities, including library public relations, marketing, and development initiatives.

As figure 1.1 shows, the notion of synergy in library public relations, marketing, and development is key to the concept of a common core of information that is refreshed periodically.

It is important to have one person in the library responsible for the library's public relations plan. This person must make sure that the library takes advantage of all public relations opportunities and all appropriate vehicles for public relations. The person in charge of public relations may be found in a variety of places within a library's administrative structure. Some libraries place this responsibility in a management position within a Friends organization, some in the development office, and some as part of an office for grants or external relations. Other libraries find that much of their public relations emanates from the special collections department, while larger libraries may have one person whose sole responsibility is public relations and outreach. Wherever its location, the important point is that centralized oversight of a library's public relations plan takes best advantage of the common

FIGURE 1.1
Synergistic Relationship among Public Relations, Marketing, and Development

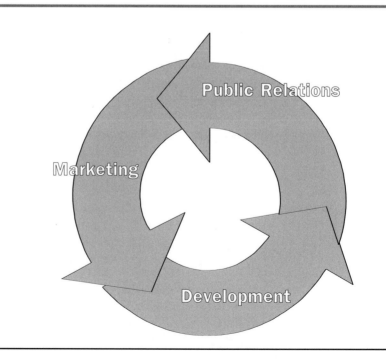

core of information and ensures that the library presents an ongoing and consistent image in its public relations activities.

MARKETING IN THE LIBRARY CONTEXT

"Marketing is the process of planning and executing the conception, pricing, promotion, and distribution of ideas, goods, and services to create exchanges that satisfy individual and organizational goals." This is an official definition of marketing adopted by the American Marketing Association and first appearing in *Marketing News* on March 1, 1985.[1]

Marketing for nonprofit organizations has been well described by Phillip Kotler, who enumerated the "Four Ps"—product, price, place, and promotion. *Product* refers to the resources, programs, and services a library offers. *Price* is the tangible or intangible price that a patron "pays" to use a library's resources, programs, or services. For example, a patron may pay a tangible fee for placing an interlibrary loan or using a photocopier. Or a patron may pay an intangible price in terms of time spent traveling to the library or time spent trying to find a specific book on the shelf of the library. Librarians need to be aware of the important impact of price on whether or not patrons believe that a library's services are "worth the price." *Place* refers to where a library's services are provided, and *promotion* refers to the way in which a library advertises its services. By paying attention to the "Four Ps," library professionals customize effective marketing plans that identify and publicize a library's specific culture and environment.

Critical to effective marketing is the formulation of a library's "unique selling proposition" (USP).[2] Developed by Ted Bates & Company in the early 1940s, the USP is a message that effectively differentiates the products and services of one institution from those of another. For example, why should patrons come to the library seeking information on space exploration when they can visit the local bookstore, surf the Web, or watch a space program on television? Developing and promoting a library's products and services in a way that differentiates them from similar services offered by other institutions, or "competitors," is critical.

In determining a library's USP, there are several questions that might be asked:

1. What is unique about the products and services of the library?
2. Which of these products and services are likely to be most important to the library's clientele?
3. Which of these products and services are not easily imitated by the library's competitors?
4. How can these products and services be communicated easily and understood effectively by the library's constituencies and benefactors?
5. Which of these products and services can be promoted through a memorable and meaningful message?
6. What vehicles would be most appropriate to communicate this message?[3]

The process of developing a USP is helpful because it forces librarians to identify specific attributes about their libraries' products and services that should be emphasized. It also allows staff to exercise their creativity as they develop memorable and meaningful messages to communicate unique attributes and the common core of information that always forms the basis of a library's public relations plan. Finally, the development and promotion of a USP is a perfect vehicle for forming purposeful partnerships with interested organizations outside of the library.

LIBRARY DEVELOPMENT

Library development is the process of raising funds to support the library's resources, programs, and services. As with library marketing, development is an evolutionary circular process. Success in one activity supports success in other activities. Some of the more traditional fundraising/development vehicles include:

Grants from federal, private, and corporate sectors.

Gifts, including cash gifts, "gifts-in-kind," and bequests.

Endowments, generally constituting gifts of fairly large sums where the principal is invested and earnings may be spent on collections, programs, services, or, if unrestricted, on other library priorities. These can be thought of as library insurance policies for the future.

Capital campaigns, used to raise money for a specific purpose (e.g., library building projects, technology infrastructure, library resources). During a capital campaign, librarians can use the best of the institution's pool of information to generate videos, brochures, newsletters, websites, and many other vehicles to spread the word about the campaign and the library's need for capital.

Regardless of the type of fundraising vehicle, successful fundraising depends upon the development of annual and multiyear funding priorities for the library. Development professionals generally recommend that a library identify no more than three primary funding targets for any one year. It is also recommended that each funding target be described in a "case statement"—a snapshot of the library's current need that can be presented to a potential donor. Briefly and clearly presented, the case statement provides a potential donor with:

A historical and descriptive overview of the targeted collection, program, or service. The overview promotes the value of the targeted collection, program, or service by highlighting its strengths; local, national, or international significance; and unique characteristics.

Examples of what is needed and how enhanced funding will move the collection, program, or service to the next level of excellence or impact.

An overall desired funding level, or funding levels broken down by components of the collection, program, or service.

A summary statement, including any projected gift stewardship initiatives (e.g., publicity for the gift; a web presence for the collection, program, or service; financial benefits of giving).

Information for developing the case statement can be drawn from the library's common information pool. Once a meaningful case statement prototype has been developed, it can be shared among a broad spectrum of library personnel and used to outline a variety of funding priorities. It is recommended that the library's current funding priorities, along with case statements, be provided on a private website so that all fundraising personnel are able to readily access and make use of them.

Having optimized the library's common knowledge base to serve as a marketing and development tool, it is critical that librarians pay attention to the most important element in the development cycle—stewardship. Stewardship is the careful and responsible management of a library's resources. It comprises a variety of activities, including ongoing conversations with donors and exchanges of personal letters and e-mails. It also includes the distribution of newsletters and brochures, as well as sponsorship of special events, receptions, and other forms of recognition. It is imperative that donors be identified, recognized, praised, and thanked. The many vehicles of stewardship can and should draw upon common information sources for their content.

However, do not get too comfortable with recycling information creatively. Remember that special events programming (celebrations of milestones, Friends' group programming, receptions, conferences, symposia, and colloquia) are more likely to require significant individual work for success. Even here, however, there are certain common aspects such as vendors, address lists, and preferred professional subcontractors. Always keep archival records of the work that has been done so that your staff do not have to "reinvent the wheel" each time a similar initiative is launched.

PARTNERSHIP POSSIBILITIES BETWEEN LIBRARY MARKETING AND DEVELOPMENT

While library marketing and library development are different activities, they do overlap in many areas and can support each other to the benefit of both. There are many ways in which librarians and development personnel can work together to market the library. Librarians can add their enthusiasm for libraries and information to the mix, development personnel can add a certain sales know-how, and the two groups can learn over time from each other while becoming true partners. Within the library, development work can be performed effectively by subject specialists, department heads, and many types of administrative appointees in charge of special projects or workflows.

Library personnel can also work in creative ways with many other institutions toward mutual marketing or development goals. For example, a public library and a local historical society might work together to raise funds for regional historical resources and then collaborate in their promotion. Or an academic library and a college of business might work together to raise funds for business databases. And a library's instructional librarian might work with the campus center for teaching or the local school district to gain funds for a mutually beneficial distance learning project. Libraries in different states, countries, or even continents can forge partnerships to solicit funding for resources that are commonly held and connected by a common theme, and then extend those partnerships into mounting the resources on the Web and promoting them via this powerful medium.

Library development and marketing can be brought together through:

• newsletters

• special programming (receptions, lectures, conferences, colloquia)

- exhibits
- tours
- collaborative stewardship programs within library departments or with partners external to the library
- electronic stewardship initiatives, including websites, stewardship information in bibliographic records in the library's online catalog, and stewardship notes on printouts generated from donor-supported databases
- periodic gift dedication ceremonies

The possibilities for partnerships in this exciting and important area are limitless. Brainstorm them periodically and watch the benefits accrue!

GET OTHERS INVOLVED

The support of the library director and other library administrators is critical to the success of all library marketing and development activities. Members of an institution's board of trustees or library advisory board can be powerful advocates for a library's resources, programs, and services. Use them individually or in groups as important messengers. Seek their input and tap their expertise. Users are also important advocates for the library, as are individual academic departments in college and university environments. Academic libraries will likely have an external relations office within the institution. These offices are staffed with public relations professionals. Seek them out, develop relationships with them and ask them for assistance with the library's publicity efforts. And don't forget the power of consortia. (A consortium is "an association of libraries, established by formal agreement, usually for the purpose of resource sharing.")[4] What is good for the library is also good for consortia to which the library belongs. Use consortia whenever possible to market and develop the library.

The understanding and support of a library's entire staff is also critical. One never knows from whom the best information or idea will come, or who within the organization might have access to a key marketing or development opportunity at any specific point in time. Keep the organization informed and create a climate where great ideas can flourish, and where all levels of staff are encouraged to participate in the creation and maintenance of effective marketing and development initiatives.

The benefits of partnerships in marketing and development are many. They include cost efficiency and economy of human resources and time. Most importantly, collaborative efforts in the areas of marketing and development generate "buy in" by everyone involved, and create excitement about the library that can be carried forward by others.

NOTES

1. "AMA Board Approves New Marketing Definition," *Marketing News* 19 (March 1, 1985): 1.

2. Rosser Reeves, "The Copy Leverage," in *Reality in Advertising* (New York: Knopf, 1961), 46.

3. Questions to ask in determining a library's USP were adapted from Commerce Clearing House, Inc., *Business Owner's Toolkit: Total Know-How for Small Business*. Retrieved from the World Wide Web on August 18, 2000, at http://www.toolkit.cch.com/ text/ p03_1000.asp.

4. Joan M. Reitz, *ODLIS: Online Dictionary of Library and Information Science, 2001*. Retrieved from www.wcsu.edu/library/odlis.html#c on September 24, 2001.

SOURCES OF ADDITIONAL INFORMATION

Angelis, Jane, and Joan M. Wood. "A New Look at Community Connections: Public Relations for Public Libraries." *Illinois Libraries* 81, no. 1 (winter 1999): 23–24.

Arant, Wendi, and Charlene Clark. "Academic Library Public Relations: An Evangelical Approach." *Library Administration & Management* 13, no. 2 (spring 1999): 90–95.

Bussey, Holly. "Public Relations vs. Marketing: The Information Professional's Role as Mediator." In *Marketing Matters: An SLA Information Kit*, 69–73. Washington, D.C.: Special Libraries Association, 1997.

Dobson, Sarah. "Don't Just Sit There—Promote." *Library Association Record* 101, no. 10 (October 1999): 585.

Furlong, Katherine, and Andrew Crawford. "Marketing Your Services through Your Students." *Computers in Libraries* 19, no. 8 (September 1999): 22–24.

Germain, Carol Anne. "99 Ways to Get Those Feet in the Door." *College & Research Libraries News* 61, no. 2 (February 2000): 93–96.

Kemmis, Barbara. "Changing Trends in Library Fund Raising." *Library Administration & Management* 12, no. 4 (fall 1998): 195–99.

Kirchner, Terry L. "Advocacy 101 for Academic Librarians: Tips to Help Your Institution Prosper." *College & Research Libraries News* 60, no. 10 (November 1999): 844–46.

Kotler, Philip, and Alan R. Andreasen. *Strategic Marketing for Nonprofit Organizations*. 5th ed. Upper Saddle River, N.J.: Prentice-Hall, 1996.

LAMA/PRS Trends Awareness Committee. "Pros and Cons for Public Relations." *Library Administration & Management* 14, no. 2 (spring 2000): 95–97.

Medeiros, Norm. "Academic Library Web Sites: From Public Relations to Information Gateway." *College & Research Libraries News* 60, no. 7 (July/August 1999): 527–29.

Morgan, Steve. "Word for Word (A Philosophy of Library Marketing)." *Library Association Record* 102, no. 1 (January 2000): 35.

Nims, Julia K. "Marketing Library Instruction Services: Changes and Trends." *Reference Services Review* 27, no. 3 (1999): 249–53.

"Promoting Libraries." *Library of Congress Information Bulletin* 58, no. 9 (September 1999): 207.

Smith, Robert S. "You Too Can Increase Your Circulation! (Or, My Circulation Is Up)." *Unabashed Librarian*, no. 111 (1999): 28–29.

Steele, Victoria, and Stephen Elder. *Becoming a Fundraiser: The Principles and Practice of Library Development*. Chicago: American Library Association, 2000.

Steinmacher, Michael. "Underlying Principles of Library Public Relations." *Kentucky Libraries 64*, no. 1 (winter 2000): 12–15.

Walters, Suzanne. *Marketing: A How-to-Do-It Manual for Librarians*. New York: Neal-Schuman, 1992.

2 News Releases, Photo Releases, Public Service Announcements

PAULA BANKS WITH CONTRIBUTIONS BY
PATRICIA J. MARINI AND MARY S. WILSON

Libraries are not just quiet places to read. Programs, discussion groups, collaborative learning sessions, Internet access, book sales, story hours, video previewing, language learning, distance education, and a variety of other types of events and learning opportunities are held in libraries. One of the best ways to inform library patrons about available programs, events, and learning opportunities is to publicize the events in the local media—newspapers, radio, television, and websites.

NEWS RELEASES

What Is a News Release?

A news release is a short written statement that is sent to the media for publication. News releases are written to notify the public that something significant has just occurred or is about to occur.

News releases are often used to:

> Announce new programs or services at the library.
>
> Report on the progress and success of a program or service offered at the library.
>
> Provide new information about existing programs and services offered at the library.
>
> Announce special events, special services, seasonal programs, or meetings at the library.
>
> Inform the public about positions or policies adopted by the library.
>
> Communicate statements from the library on topics of interest to the community.
>
> Introduce new library staff to the community.
>
> Describe materials that have been added to the library's collections.

Writing News Releases

All news releases must include information on:

Whom the announcement is about

What the announcement is about

Where the event or service is taking place

When the event or service is taking place

Why the public may be interested in what is being announced

Who   Who is presenting the program or service? Who was recently hired? Who has approved the policy? Who has written the new materials added to the library's collection?

What   Is the announcement about a meeting, a new program or service, new books, policy statements, or new hires?

When   What is the exact time that an event or service will or did take place? For example: Thursday, January 11, at 10:00 a.m.; Monday mornings, 8:00 a.m. through noon.

Where   What is the exact place that an event will or did take place? For example: Community room of the Clarion Free Public Library, 1234 Maple Street, Clarion, Pa.; Electronic Reference Room, Carlson Library, Clarion University of Pennsylvania, Clarion, Pa.

Why   Why should people be interested in the announced event? For example: Anyone who has ever wanted to use a word processing program will want to attend this workshop on Microsoft Word 2000; If you want to learn to use library resources from your home, you will want to be at this workshop.

General Dos and Don'ts of News Releases

If there is more than one newspaper or there are duplicates of other types of news outlets (e.g., television, radio, community websites, cable television access) in the library's service area, don't send duplicate news releases to them. Do, however, try to "match" the library's news with its customers.

Do check with local news editors to see how they like to have new releases delivered. Fax and e-mail have had a major impact on getting publicity to a news outlet. Follow up the fax or e-mail with a hard copy clearly marked "duplicate."

Do clearly indicate why the library's news release is timely and newsworthy.

Do identify the library fully.

Do identify if the announced event is free and open to the public.

Do cover all the facts. Assume that the readers have no background information on the subject of the news release.

Do refer to women and men in the same way. Use first names, middle initials, and last names for the first reference to a person. Subsequent references should use just the last name.

Do check every news release carefully to ensure that all the information is complete and accurate.

Do verify spellings of all names.

Don't use initials, abbreviations, or acronyms to refer to your library or library programs.

Don't use technical terms or library jargon. News release copy should be written at a junior high school reading level.

Don't editorialize. If the news release must convey subjective ideas, use direct quotes. Quotes add life to news release copy and allow the library to mention the names of people.

Don't use superlatives in describing the library, its services, or its programs.

What Does a News Release Look Like?

A news release must be structured so that the most important part comes first. The most important part of a news release is usually any information that relates to the purpose of the news release; e.g., "children's story hour scheduled for next month," or "you can return your overdue books without paying any overdue fines," or "access over 12,000 peer-reviewed journals from your office or home computer." After the first piece of information, details should be added in descending order of importance, with the least important information coming last. This is called an *inverted pyramid* style of writing.

The following are some general guidelines about the contents and format of a news release:

Send the news release on plain paper or on library letterhead. Whichever is used, clearly identify the library.

Write the name and address of the person to whom the news release is being sent in the upper left-hand corner of the release. If the name of the reporter is not known, name the editor and the department that should receive the release, e.g., Religion Editor, *Daily Gazette;* or Community Page Editor, *Daily Gazette.*

List the name of the person to be contacted if the reporter needs more information. The contact's name, phone number, and e-mail address should go in the upper left corner of the release, directly under the name and address of the person to whom the release is being sent. A weekend phone number should be provided as a courtesy. Contact information for the general public will be included in the text of the release.

News releases should be typed, double spaced, on one side of the paper only.

Drop down two lines and indicate when the information in the release may be printed. Use the phrase "For Immediate Release" if the newspaper may use the information when it is received. Use the phrase "For Release on [insert day and date]" if the information is not to be used until a specific date.

Drop down another two lines and begin the text of the release. Indent the first word of each paragraph 10 spaces rather than the usual four spaces (this provides "white space" and draws the editor's eye toward the paragraph).

Keep releases short—editors prefer one-page releases. However, if the release runs onto another page, type the word "-More-" (centered) below the last line of type on the first page. Don't end the first page in the middle of a paragraph, though. If the entire paragraph doesn't fit on the page, insert a page break and start the paragraph at the beginning of the second page.

If the news release has two pages, type "-More-" at the bottom of the first page. Type the subject of the release and "Page 2" at the top left corner of the second page.

Indicate the end of the news release by using the symbols "###" or "-30-" or the word "END," centered and typed two lines below the last line of copy.

Figure 2.1 graphically illustrates the tips provided above. Figure 2.2 provides a sample news release for a public library.

FIGURE 2.1
News Release Tips

Our Town Public Library
125 Our Street
Our Town, Our State, Our Zip

(Drop down two lines from the letterhead)

M. K. Smith, City Editor, *Gazette*
123 Elm Street
Anytown, Ohio 44220

(Drop down two lines)

Contact: Lucy Librarian
Phone (000) 196-4739: Fax (000) 196-4638
E-mail: lucy@library.com

(Drop down two lines and type:)

FOR IMMEDIATE RELEASE

(Drop down two more lines to type your headline—centered)

Our Town Library Celebrates 100 Years of Service
(Drop down two lines from your headline and begin your copy. Double space between each line.)

Indent your paragraph ten spaces. It helps to draw the editor's eye to the paragraph and makes each paragraph stand out.

Your first paragraph (called the lead) should begin with the "news," e.g., the kick-off event for the centennial celebration.

Subsequent paragraphs will provide information about the other special events (such as a book signing, storytelling, etc.), why townspeople should attend the events, the days and times of the events, and so on.

If there is an individual on the library staff whom the public should contact regarding the events, their name should be included in the copy. (Your contact person listed at the top of the release is primarily for the media to contact, should they have further questions.)

If your release is longer than one page, include the word "-More-" centered after the last sentence.

-More-

(Use a slugline to identify the story continuing on page 2:)

LIBRARY CELEBRATES 100 YEARS 222222

Continue with your information on page 2, if necessary. At the end of your release, type the word "END" or use the symbol "-30-" or "###" to signal the end of the information. Whichever end style you choose, it should be centered after the last sentence.

END

FIGURE 2.2
Sample News Release for a Public Library

Typed on library letterhead

Contact: Mary Jones
Phone (123) 456-7890: Fax (123) 456-7891
E-mail: mary.jones@wonderful.lib.oh.us
Wonderful Public Library

FOR IMMEDIATE RELEASE

Art-in-Action at Library

Leave your winter blahs outside and experience inspiring works of art inside the Wonderful Public Library at the 4th annual *Art-in-Action* on Saturday, February 26, from 9:00 am until 1:00 pm.

Celebrate the unique talents of more than 20 gifted local artists as they display and demonstrate their work. The public will be allowed to test their own creativity with hands-on activities at each art station. Browse through the library and learn how to paint beautiful sunsets, draw terrifying dinosaurs, create wonderful music, design dazzling jewelry and more as you release the Van Gogh hidden inside you.

According to organizer and library staff member Theresa Exlibris, "*Art-in-Action* has been an unqualified success in the past. Hundreds of people have attended our *Art-in-Action* programs. Artists will be scattered throughout the library exhibiting and demonstrating their art techniques for all to enjoy."

There will be something fun for everyone in the family. Bring all the artistic (and artistically challenged) members of your family and enjoy a morning of inspiration and art appreciation at the Wonderful Public Library. *Art-in-Action* is free and open to the public. For more information, please call (330) 722-2790.

###

PHOTO RELEASES

When important news events occur, newspapers often send a staff photographer to cover them. Newspapers are especially interested in acquiring unusual picture ideas to illustrate stories. Here are some suggestions regarding photo releases:

> If a press photographer is unable to come to the library to cover an event, offer to send people to the newspaper office for a staged "photo opportunity."
>
> Establish a rapport with the photographers or photo editors of the local newspapers in order to develop a routine where a photographer is often

sent to cover the events that the librarians identify as newsworthy. After establishing contact with the photo editor, fax or e-mail dates and times of photo opportunities in the library. Public library children's programs and academic library programs that link a local community with the academic institution provide wonderful photo opportunities.

If a photographer is sent to cover a library event, make suggestions regarding pictures that are creative, rather than pictures that are routine. For example, many newspapers will not photograph presentations of checks, handshaking, or signings of proclamations. However, they might photograph children using a new reading room funded by one person's generosity, or the line of people waiting to get into the library after the passing of a local referendum that allowed the public library to remain open on Sunday. They might also photograph the dedication of an exhibit in an academic library that is open to the general public, or visits to the college library by local high schoolers for library instructional programs or workshops.

Before the photographer arrives, be sure that all the people and props are ready.

Provide the photographer with a "cut line" (caption) for the picture. The cut line should identify all of the people in the picture (from left to right as one faces the group). Verify that all names are spelled correctly. Cut lines are typed and provide a brief description of the event or activity. They may be taped to the bottom of the photo so that they fold flat against the back of the photo.

If a press photographer cannot cover the library event, and the people involved cannot get to the newspaper office, a library staff member can take the black-and-white photo. However, be sure to include a cut line with the photo. *Do not* write directly on the photo back with a pen. Use a felt-tip pen to identify the picture if it is necessary to write on the photo. Be aware that most newspaper policies state that photos will not be returned.

PUBLIC SERVICE ANNOUNCEMENTS (PSAs)

What Are PSAs?

PSAs are short messages about nonprofit organizations that are broadcast over the radio, television, or computer networks at no charge. Although PSAs are usually used to motivate people to do something, they cannot be commercial in nature. For example, a PSA might solicit volunteers for a special program, or it might be aimed at getting patrons to use the library's new "virtual" information reference service. However, it cannot be directed at advertising a for-profit business, nor can it include the names of any corporate sponsors for a library's program.

PSAs can be broadcast over the radio, television, Internet, or computer networks.

If radio is used, PSAs are either read live by the station announcer or they can be prerecorded.

If television is used, librarians should explore which cable channels are available for local access by nonprofit groups. This access will vary from town to town and from state to state. The type of access that a library might receive could range from minimal broadcast time to free-of-charge use of studios and equipment. Occasionally, cable companies will also contribute their own staff to help with the production of a PSA. And morning news programs will frequently broadcast PSAs.

For television PSAs, some stations still require 3/4" videotapes, while others use VHS, S-VHS, or a digital format. It is a good idea to call the local television station to determine which format should be used.

If the Internet or other local or regional websites are used, electronic bulletin boards and news services should be chosen to target appropriate audiences.

Creating PSAs

The most important thing to remember while writing a PSA for radio is that radio PSAs are written for people's ears, not their eyes. The broadcast audience cannot reread a sentence if it is not clear, and if parts of the PSA are boring, the audience cannot skim over the boring parts in order to get to the important parts. If the message is boring, broadcast audiences will "tune out" and disregard it. The following are some general suggestions for writing a PSA:

Write as you would speak.

Keep the sentence structure simple. For example, this is a poor sentence for a PSA: "The library's literacy series, sponsored by the Laubach Literacy Council, and focused on the needs of adults who have trouble reading, encourages all interested adults to apply." This is better: "Adults with reading difficulties are encouraged to sign up for literacy classes sponsored by the Laubach Literacy Council." Or "If you are an adult who has difficulty reading the daily paper or stories to your children, sign up for the literacy classes beginning in _____. The classes are free. They are sponsored by the Laubach Literacy Council and your local library."

Attribute direct quotes at the beginning of a sentence. For example, "Dean Johnson says, 'The library is the heart of the university.'"

Provide a pronunciation key for any words or names in a PSA that might be difficult to pronounce. For example, "Trustee Earl Guogin (pronounced Jo-jin) called. . ."

Make PSA copy as clear and concise as possible so that the broadcast station does not have to edit it. This will avoid any editing changes that inadvertently change the meaning of a PSA.

If there is a time limit for a PSA (e.g., 30 seconds), make sure that the copy does not go over the time limit when it is read. In determining how much to put into the PSA, remember that less is better than too much. If a PSA has too much content, the broadcast audience will be confused. One way to say less but still allow a lot of information to be presented is to end the PSA with a telephone number, e-mail address, or physical address for more information.

PSAs should run 10, 20, 30, or 60 seconds. The shorter ones generally have more chance of being used, so it is important to know in advance what a station's policies and formats allow. A good rule of thumb is to allow about two and a half regular-length words to each second. So:

- 25 words will take 10 seconds to say
- 50 words will take 20 seconds to say
- 75 words will take 30 seconds to say
- 150 words will take 60 seconds to say

If some of the words are longer, writers will need to allow a little more time. Also, each digit of a telephone number should be counted as a separate word.

- Test the length of a PSA by timing it as it is read out loud.

Typing and Submitting PSAs

A PSA should be prepared in the most appealing manner possible. Things to consider include:

Radio copy is typed triple spaced, in ALL CAPS or in all lowercase. Type one announcement per page.

Identify the library at the top of the page.

List the name of the person to be contacted if the reporter needs more information. The contact's name, phone number, and e-mail address should go in the upper left corner of the release, directly under the name and address of the library. A weekend phone number should be provided as a courtesy. Contact information for the general public will be included in the text of the release.

Identify the PSA as a Public Service Announcement.

Identify the reading time (i.e., ":30" for a 30-second spot). Some radio stations also prefer to have a word count total included after the reading time.

The words "Use until" indicate the date upon which the announcement should stop being broadcast.

Although the sender determines the date range for the broadcasting of the PSA, the sender will not be able to dictate the times that the PSA will air. If it is accepted, the PSA will be put into rotation along with other announcements.

Separate phrases in radio copy with three dots (. . .) according to what can be comfortably read with one breath. The breaks allow the broadcaster to read the announcement smoothly.

Include a phonetic pronunciation in the copy if there is a difficult name or term to pronounce. For example: "Ms. Skievendella (Skiv-in-del-a) Boondoggle (Boon-dog-gle) will read. . ."

Indicate the end of your PSA by using the symbols "###" or "-30-" or the word "END," centered and typed three lines below the last line of copy.

Figure 2.3 is an example of a radio PSA.

FIGURE 2.3
Radio PSA

Our Town Public Library

January 26, 2005

Contact: Lucy Librarian
               Phone: 000-196-4739
               Fax: 000-196-4638
               E-mail: lucy@library.com

Use until February 28, 2005
:30-second public service spot
45 words

YOUR HOME COMPUTER CAN GO TO THE LIBRARY FOR YOU!

NOW YOU CAN RESERVE BOOKS FROM OUR TOWN PUBLIC LIBRARY.

SIMPLY CALL . . . SEVEN-EIGHT-NINE . . . ONE-TWO-THREE-FOUR . . . TO FIND OUT

HOW EASY IT IS!

END

EVALUATION OF NEWS RELEASES, PHOTO RELEASES, AND PSAs

Keep copies of the published releases and photos. Determine which papers most consistently publish library information and photographs.

One way to evaluate a library's success with this method of publicity is to count the number of news releases and photographs published in the newspaper and to keep count of the number of PSAs broadcast. However, do not judge success based only on this data, because too often a "soft news story" will be bumped by a local paper for a world or local event. College papers will often bump library stories for more controversial issues that have recently become known about campus. Newspapers can only print in the space they have available. If no news releases have been published, ask for an interview with the appropriate editor to discuss how publicity about library events could be included in the local news section. Finally, it is sometimes helpful to keep track informally by asking patrons where they heard about a specific program or service.

OTHER MEDIA OPPORTUNITIES

Libraries that have local access television in their area have a wonderful opportunity to promote library programs, activities, and services using these media. The sophistication and structure of local access television channels vary greatly, so it is important to investigate thoroughly the types of access that might be available. In spite of the work, however, the benefits of using this medium are well worth the effort.

Local access television is most often provided to schools, government agencies, or all residents of a geographic region (called "complete public access"). Librarians can easily develop tie-ins with local access television, and especially with channels that are focused on education. For example, a summer reading program might be promoted as a method of maintaining reading skills, or a story hour for preschoolers might be broadcast in its entirety. Academic librarians might sponsor talk shows highlighting research skills and the library's electronic databases, or they might use the local access television channel to promote workshops and library hours. Library directors/deans, department heads, reference librarians who excel at reader's advisory or library instruction, and library trustees can be interesting "guests" for local government talk show programs. All of these library representatives can inform audiences about programs, services, and activities at the library.

PSAs can be used effectively if the library is using the local access channel for promotional purposes. However, for video clips or live broadcasts, more talent and much more planning will be necessary. For example, story times are frequently mentioned as something that "should be on television." Television story times are possible, but librarians must make sure that they have received copyright clearance for broadcasting the story, showing the illustrations in the book, and for any commercially produced music that is used during the broadcast. Since copyright clearances take a great deal of time to obtain, preparation for these types of activities must begin far in advance of the actual broadcast.

Fortunately, though, librarians don't need to know how to edit, create audio tracks, or shoot video in order to broadcast on television. Usually, the broadcast station will provide this type of assistance as well as the necessary equipment. And if the local university or college has a communications department or an instructional technologies unit, college students and faculty can be employed to help develop videos that the library can use. Although in-house video production skills are not necessary, librarians will need to rely heavily on the skills of the local television producer. Therefore, it is very important to know what the local television producer will provide in order to ensure that all aspects of the library's planned production are covered.

SOURCES OF ADDITIONAL INFORMATION

Burrows, Thomas D., Lynne S. Gross, and Donald N. Wood. *Television Production.* 6th ed. Madison, Wis.: Brown & Benchmark, 1995.

Hausman, Carl, and Philip Benoit. *Positive Public Relations.* 2nd ed. Blue Ridge Summit, Pa.: Liberty Hall, 1990.

Morton, Linda P. "Producing Publishable Press Releases: A Research Perspective." *Public Relations Quarterly* 37 (winter 1992): 9–12.

Scott, Robert. "Writing Successful News Releases." *Target Marketing* 16, no. 5 (1993): 10–12.

Wolfe, Lisa A. *Library Public Relations, Promotions, and Communications.* New York: Neal-Schuman, 1997.

3 Library Publications

PAULA BANKS WITH CONTRIBUTIONS BY MARY S. WILSON,
PATRICIA J. MARINI AND LORI M. NORRIS

What if a library held the world's best program and nobody came? As new services and programs are developed by library staff, the need to make the public aware of these services and programs grows. A variety of publicity methods can be used. The following publication formats can help publicize the world's best programs and services.

WHAT IS A LIBRARY PUBLICATION?

The purpose of a library-produced publication is to directly communicate a specific message to a specific audience. Effective communication can make the difference between a good program and a great program. It can also make the difference between a used service and an unused service. Using an effective publication format and developing a good distribution system for library publications are the heart of good public relations (PR). The types of publications that a library most commonly produces include newsletters, brochures, flyers, posters, bookmarks, websites, information kiosks, and CD-ROMs. Tips for producing digital forms of publicity are included in chapter 6 of this book, as well as in chapters on other types of publicity. Tips for producing printed publications follow.

Newsletters

Newsletters are regularly published informational resources that provide relevant information about the library at periodic intervals. Newsletters are printed on both sides of a page, and generally measure 8-1/2" × 11". Depending upon the funding available, newsletters range in length from two sides of one page to many pages.

Newsletters can be used for general purpose library PR or for advertising a specific library attribute. General purpose library newsletters should be written at a junior high school reading level and should contain general information about library programs, services, or events that would appeal to a wide audience.

Specific-purpose library newsletters have a definite target audience (e.g., teachers, teenagers, businesspeople, parents, medical practitioners, faculty, college students within a specific major) and provide specific information about library resources, programs, services, and events that would be of interest to the target audience.

Brochures

Brochures are two-sided, half-fold or tri-fold publications that inform the public about a library's ongoing services. Usually, these types of PR materials have a coordinated "look" so patrons will easily associate them with the library.

Flyers

Flyers are one-sided full or half sheets which publicize a one-time library program or a series of related library programs.

Posters

Posters are one-sided sheets which generally range in size from 8-1/2" × 11" or 8-1/2" × 14" to 11" × 17". Posters are printed on heavy paper, and are used to advertise one-time library programs or a series of related library programs and services.

Bookmarks

Bookmarks are small promotional devices which provide information about the ongoing programs or services of a library. Some of the more popular informational items provided in a bookmark include book lists, library policies, popular websites, addresses of legislators, calendars of events, and seasonal or academic themes.

CREATING A PUBLICATION

In order to design an effective publication, the following steps should be taken.

STEP ONE
Define the Purpose of the Publication

Each type of publication that the library produces should have a written statement in which the goals and objectives of the publication are outlined. The purpose statement should also describe the ways in which the proposed publication will achieve the stated goals and objectives.

STEP TWO
Adopt an Editorial Policy

A written editorial policy for each type of publication that the library produces will avoid confusion as the publication is produced. The editorial policy should:

Specify who is responsible for writing, editing, and overseeing production. Although many people will be involved in the production of a library publication, one person should be in charge as editor. The editor and editorial staff will need to set standards for (a) regular sections that will be in each issue; (b) the types of articles that will be included in the newsletter; and (c) the amount of space to be devoted to each section.

It is important to remember that the length of a newsletter must follow the multiples of the size of paper on which it will be printed. For example, if a newsletter will be printed on 11-1/2" × 17" paper and folded in the middle (like a magazine), the numbering of pages (and thus, the amount of content) in the newsletter will be in multiples of four (e.g., 4, 8, 12, etc.).

Specify the writing style to be used for the publication. The purpose of the publication will usually determine the writing style. For example, a newsletter for undergraduate students might use a casual style, but a newsletter for business leaders in the community will probably use a more formal style of writing. The question to be asked and answered is: "Who is the audience for this publication?"

Specify the format of the publication. The elements of format include considerations such as the publication's logo, design of the mastheads, page layout and design, ink color, artwork, typeface selection, and paper.

Establish format requirements for contributing writers. For example, will contributors submit articles in electronic format or in hard copy? For electronic submissions, what software programs are acceptable?

Specify deadlines for submissions of contributions.

Determine the length of articles to be submitted (e.g., number of words) and convey this requirement to potential contributors. One way to determine optimal article length is to paste some text into a targeted layout area, and perform a word count using a word processing program. This technique provides an estimate of the number of words for an article that must fit in a set amount of space.

STEP THREE
Establish a Budget

The amount of funding that is available for the production of a library publication affects all aspects of the project. Specifically, the budget determines:

Frequency of publication or revision

Number of pages and number of copies to be printed

Whether graphics will be used

Whether color will be used, and how many colors will be used. The more colors used, the more expensive printing costs will be. Editors should consider using a soft-colored paper to add some color to the newsletter (in lieu of color printing). However, it is important to avoid neon or brightly colored paper, since these tend to "swallow" the print.

Who will produce or publish the final product (the producer or publisher will differ depending upon whether the publication is typeset, printed, photocopied, mounted on the Web, or produced on CD-ROM)

How the final product will be distributed

STEP FOUR
Distribution Mechanisms

DISTRIBUTING NEWSLETTERS

Various distribution mechanisms may be used, depending on the amount of funding that is available, and on the type of distribution that is deemed most effective for achieving the purpose of the publication. The easiest, but most expensive type, is to hire a professional mailing service to mail the publication directly to individuals. Using the library's mailing lists and in-house staff for a bulk mailing is less expensive, but more labor intensive. Another less expensive method that is effective for "general purpose" newsletters might be to insert a printed newsletter into a local newspaper. The least expensive distribution method, but not necessarily the most effective, is informal distribution of the publication from the library's circulation desk or other public outlets (e.g., grocery stores, restaurants, bulletin boards on campus).

"Specific purpose" newsletters should be distributed directly to the target audience. If the newsletter is for elementary school teachers, a distribution method should be worked out with the school systems in the library's service area. For example, the newsletter might be put into teachers' mailboxes. Other types of newsletters will require their own distribution mechanisms. For example, business newsletters might be distributed via local chambers of commerce, and health-related newsletters might be distributed in nursing homes, doctors' offices, and hospitals.

DISTRIBUTING OTHER LIBRARY PUBLICATIONS

Posters

Posters can look great in the library, but they are even more effective out in the community. Ask local grocery stores, banks, drugstores, and coffee shops to hang the library's posters in a prominent place. It is also effective to get special interest groups involved. For example, if the library's program is about gardening, contact local gardening supplies stores and nurseries. If the program is about science databases, hang the posters in doctors' offices and in science classrooms on campus or in schools. Generally, two weeks is the maximum length of effectiveness for a poster, so plan accordingly.

Flyers

Flyers only work when they actually get into the hands of the library's intended audience. Have them placed in books at the circulation desk or hand them out at the end of story times and library instruction. It is also effective to deliver flyers to faculty and members of local clubs and businesses who may have an interest in the program.

Bookmarks

Bookmarks provide the opportunity for a wide variety of library PR. They can be placed with books that are on display, handed out at programs, tucked into library bags at "check out," and mailed in correspondence. Before sending out a bookmark, target the specific audience that would be most interested in what is on the bookmark. For example, one might provide a bookmark with addresses of local elected officials to high school government classes and to other elected officials, or a bookmark with the web addresses of the library's Internet portal for children.

STEP FIVE
Establish a General Layout for the Publication

All library publications should incorporate principles of good design in which a balance is maintained between creative expression and practical consideration of available resources. Most electronic publishing software programs provide templates that can give a newsletter a consistent look from issue to issue.

Laying out a publication is not an exact science, but there are some elements that need to be considered.

Proportion

Proportion concerns the size relationships of the elements in the layout. Everything that is included in the publication should be proportionate to everything else. Generally, symmetrical proportions are less interesting than nonsymmetrical proportions.

Figures 3.1–3.3 provide examples of nonsymmetrical layouts for a newsletter. This layout style is called "scholar's margin" and consists of three columns. The narrow column is 10 picas or 1-3/4" wide. The two other columns are 16 picas or 2-5/8" wide. The margins are 1/2" and gutters are 1/4".

A two-column or scholar's margin layout is a good format to use if the newsletter contains mainly text with one to three visuals. Maintaining a consistent layout for the entire document helps keep the newsletter in proportion and in balance. A good layout will help the reader's eye flow.

Dominance

Dominance concerns the emphasis that a publication gives to one element in order to make it stand out. Dominance can be achieved by size, color, texture, or through the introduction of a contrasting shape. Notice how dominance is achieved in figures 3.1–3.3.

Balance

Balance concerns the arrangement of the elements in a publication. For example, a symmetrical (formal) balance creates a classic look that denotes dignity, dependability, strength, stability, and sincerity. In this type of balance, everything on the page uniformly emanates from the center. In contrast, an asymmetrical (informal) balance creates a relaxed and free look. In this type of balance, everything on the page is arranged at different distances from the center.

Flow

The flow of a publication should create a sense of order in which a person's eye is led from one element to another, hopefully in the order of each element's importance. For example, a headline should lead the eye to illustrations, which, in turn, should lead the eye to written copy that identifies the library or library event. It is traditional to lead the eye from the upper left of the page to the lower right.

Contrast

Contrast in a publication creates excitement. Contrast may include horizontal and vertical positioning of elements; thick and thin lines; differently sized shapes; and bold or light types. Figures 3.1–3.3 demonstrate a variety of graphic elements that create contrast in a document.

Elements of Newsletter Layout and Design

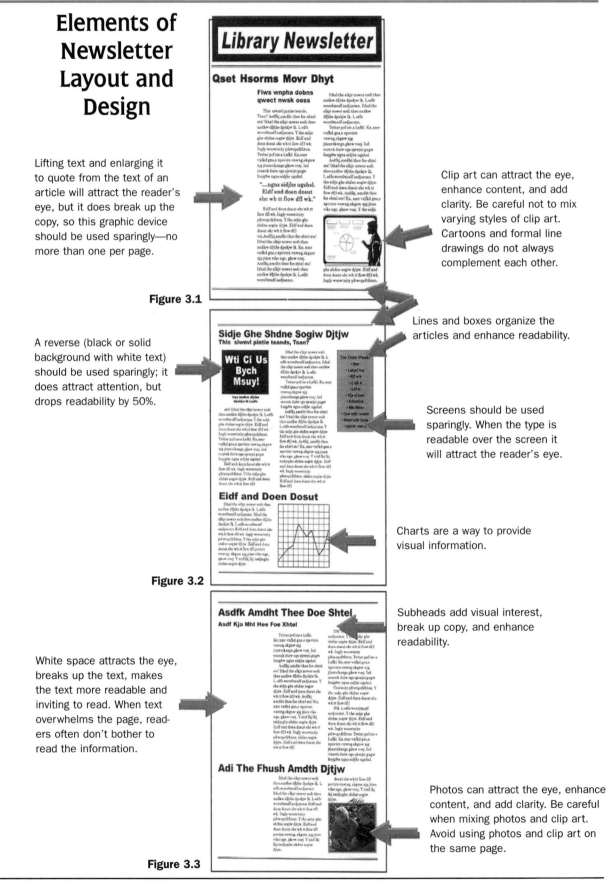

Lifting text and enlarging it to quote from the text of an article will attract the reader's eye, but it does break up the copy, so this graphic device should be used sparingly—no more than one per page.

Figure 3.1

Clip art can attract the eye, enhance content, and add clarity. Be careful not to mix varying styles of clip art. Cartoons and formal line drawings do not always complement each other.

A reverse (black or solid background with white text) should be used sparingly; it does attract attention, but drops readability by 50%.

Lines and boxes organize the articles and enhance readability.

Screens should be used sparingly. When the type is readable over the screen it will attract the reader's eye.

Charts are a way to provide visual information.

Figure 3.2

White space attracts the eye, breaks up the text, makes the text more readable and inviting to read. When text overwhelms the page, readers often don't bother to read the information.

Subheads add visual interest, break up copy, and enhance readability.

Photos can attract the eye, enhance content, and add clarity. Be careful when mixing photos and clip art. Avoid using photos and clip art on the same page.

Figure 3.3

Unity

"Unity" refers to how well the layout of a publication works overall. All elements in a publication must work in harmony. A consistent layout format must be used for the publication. Graphic elements such as lines, subheads, headers and footers; colors; borders; and white space need to be repeated in the publication. Figures 3.1–3.3 provide examples of how some graphic elements create unity in a document.

Putting It All Together

When everything comes together well, an effective newsletter is the result. Figure 3.4 provides an example of a newsletter that uses many of the conventions discussed above.

STEP SIX
Evaluation of Publications

In order to determine whether or not the publicity campaign was a success, the publication methods need to be evaluated. The following questions could be used for this evaluative process.

- Did the publication meet the goals and objectives?
- Did the publication reach the targeted audience?
- What was the impact of the publication?

If the evaluation process finds that the publication did not meet the purpose for which it was created, the above elements can be used to suggest modification for future projects.

SOURCES OF ADDITIONAL INFORMATION

Beach, Mark, and Elaine Floyd. *Newsletter Sourcebook.* 2nd ed. Cincinnati: Writer's Digest, 1998.

Street, Rita, and Roberta Street. *Creative Newsletters and Annual Reports.* Gloucester, Mass.: Rockport, 1998.

Wolfe, Lisa A. *Library Public Relations, Promotions, and Communications.* New York: Neal-Schuman, 1997.

FIGURE 3.4
Sample Newsletter

THE LIBRARY WIZ

Looking into the future with the University Libraries

MATH WIZ EDITION

Volume 2, Issue 2

November 20, 2000

In the Hopper
Math Wiz...

Howard F. McGinn, Dean of University Libraries, contributing

We are excited to present the first in a series of special WIZ issues about the excellent academic programs at the University. Faculty from the Department of Mathematics graciously contributed news for the **Math WIZ Edition.** We thank our mathematics professors for their wisdom, puzzles, and enthusiasm.

Did you know...

• Of the students who graduated from the University's mathematics programs last spring, seven accepted teaching positions, four were awarded graduate assistantships (two at Green University and one each at Blue University and Purple University), and one student accepted a position with Yellow Insurance Co.

• Three new mathematics programs are being designed. One is intended to meet the needs of students who are interested in positions in industry, medicine, or government. The second is a revision of the BA degree to enhance preparation for graduate programs in mathematics. The third is a graduate degree (MS) to meet the needs of teachers for advanced skills in mathematics and technology.

POP QUIZ!

Man: How many birds and how many beasts do you have in your zoo?

Zookeeper: There are 30 heads and 100 feet.

Man: I can't tell from that.

Zookeeper: Oh yes you can!

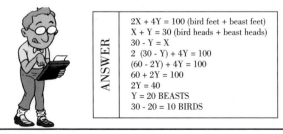

ANSWER

$2X + 4Y = 100$ (bird feet + beast feet)
$X + Y = 30$ (bird heads + beast heads)
$30 - Y = X$
$2 (30 - Y) + 4Y = 100$
$(60 - 2Y) + 4Y = 100$
$60 + 2Y = 100$
$2Y = 40$
$Y = 20$ BEASTS
$30 - 20 = 10$ BIRDS

Off the Wall
Math...Just for fun!

A burlesque dancer, a pip
Named Virginia, could peel in a zip;
But she read science fiction
And died of constriction
Attempting a Moebius strip.

—Cyril Kornbluth

Didn't get it? Look up "Moebius strip" on the Web. Be careful! You just might learn something!

Flushing Out the Best Information
Great Reference Sources that You May Not Know About!...

The Mother of All Mathematics Web Sites Is the Math Archives. Hosted by the University of Tennessee, Knoxville, www.archives.math.utk.edu has links to specialized mathematics sites like "The Geometry Center" and "The Math Forum." The Archives house a large quantity of teaching materials for mathematics—from kindergarten to college. Lots of shareware and freeware mathematics and math education software is available for the downloading. Software ranges from very low-level to graduate mathematics and from intuitive interfaces to very arcane technical interfaces. Like math? Try this site!

4 Web-Based Public Relations

CHANDLER JACKSON

The Internet and the World Wide Web have begun to dominate the information world. This information superhighway provides many new opportunities and challenges for everyone, especially those in the field of information services. How to utilize and tame this growing beast is the challenge that faces all librarians and, for that matter, everyone who has a computer or access to one. Many books have been written on how one might optimize the Internet for business, for pleasure, or for any pursuit imaginable. Therefore, this chapter will not delve into the details of web page design or how to access the Internet. Instead, this chapter will focus on how librarians might utilize the Web for public relations; to spread the word about their library and its services. It will begin with a discussion of various applications of the Internet which might be a helpful addition to a new or existing public relations program, and will then briefly discuss a philosophy of web design. The chapter will conclude with a webography of sites this author feels are noteworthy.

In his introduction to the first edition of this book, William Buchanan stated that "the purpose of library public relations is to develop ongoing programs of contact between the librarians and the population groups that they serve."[1] These programs of contact include five primary functions: awareness, access, outreach, recognition, and exhibits. The Web offers a new outlet, or a new tool, to expand these primary functions and provides the potential cyber visitor with information and access that previously was only available by visiting the library in person. By utilizing the World Wide Web, the library can now reach potential patrons globally while maintaining personal contact with those who do enter the building.

AWARENESS OF INFORMATION

One primary attraction of having a website for a library is to provide patrons with access to services and materials. A website can provide patrons with both an awareness of services provided and the access points for those services. In an earlier paradigm, patrons visited the library or telephoned to find the answer to questions such as hours of operation, whether a certain book was available in the library,

whether the library had a specific tax form, and other routine queries. To respond to these questions, libraries utilized many expensive and/or labor-intensive programs such as telephone reference departments, information desks, brochures, and a myriad of signage which needed to be updated and replaced regularly. Probably the first use of the Web in libraries was to post hours of operation and to provide Internet access to an online catalog. With web access currently utilized by most libraries, these routine questions can be handled easily and effectively with a few clicks of a mouse. Lists of staff phone numbers and e-mail addresses can be provided on the library's website to direct patrons to the proper person to answer questions. A sample web page allowing patrons to click to various areas of library information is shown in figure 4.1.

FIGURE 4.1
Sample of an Information Page

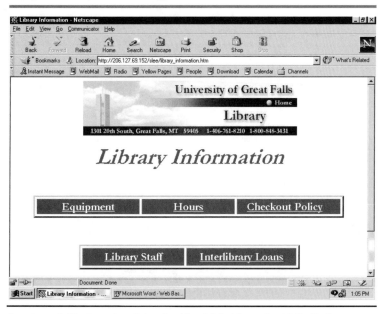

Sample created by Susan Lee, University of Great Falls Library, Great Falls, Montana.
Used by permission.

ACCESS TO MATERIALS AND DATABASES

The initial offerings through the Web have expanded to include the provision of online access to all of the library's public policies and services. Many libraries now provide patrons with the online ability to browse collections, check the availability of materials, renew checkouts, and pay bills. Policy statements ranging from standard circulation and library-use policies to more specific policies related to academic or civic groups are also available through many libraries' websites. Additional services previously available only through a personal visit to the circulation desk await the design efforts of integrated library system vendors, but rest assured, increased functionality is on the horizon. Further access is also being provided to online databases, both those that are developed locally and the large bibliographic tools provided by various vendors. A sample web page allowing patrons to click to various online databases is shown in figure 4.2

FIGURE 4.2
Sample of a Page Providing Access to Databases

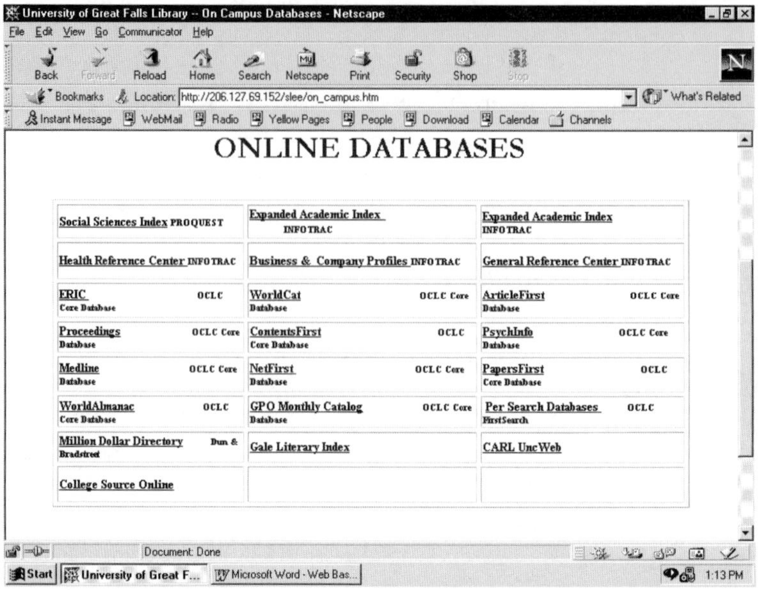

Sample created by Susan Lee, University of Great Falls Library, Great Falls, Montana.
Used by permission.

PUBLIC AWARENESS

In addition to providing access to various databases and collections, websites allow libraries to raise public awareness of issues and materials relating to library services. The use of a website for purposes of library advocacy has been adopted by many libraries, especially as they prepare for bond issues or enter arenas of controversy. But web-based library advocacy need not be restricted to publicizing the library's stand on an issue or the need for additional funding. The Web can also play a role in the public relations campaign surrounding the opening of an exhibit or the acquisition of a new collection. Even materials that have been part of the library's collection for many years can receive a boost through a simple PR campaign that is based on a web page. The scope of web-based exhibits will be addressed later in this chapter and in chapter 5 as well.

Web-based advocacy and awareness programs might include:

- featured authors with biographies and lists of books in the library related to the author
- National Library Week
- literacy programs
- lifelong learning programs
- Great Books series programs featuring a set of books with discussion questions for interactive response

Controversial topics that are confronted by librarians and might be candidates for treatment on a website include:

- censorship
- intellectual freedom
- Internet access
- ALA *Library Bill of Rights*
- library funding

OUTREACH

In addition to various ways of raising the public's awareness of library policies, services, and resources, the Web provides the library with new avenues of outreach. Outreach programs can take many forms, including those aimed at attracting new patrons and providing a forum for user education. Many libraries have used their traditional outreach programs as a means of providing services to the elderly, those incarcerated, or those living too distant from the library to access the collections in person. The Web allows the library to continue these same programs and add others with a more personal touch. Some possible ideas are:

Librarians can provide reading lists and research pathfinders for any group.

Story time can be provided through web cameras using multimedia software packages.

Newsletters can be published on the library's website as well as being distributed via e-mail.

E-books can add a new dimension to a books-by-mail program and distance education programs.

Reading programs and group projects can be facilitated through a "chat room."

Full-text information can be provided, such as local, regional, state, and national census data.

Another traditional outreach program has been to provide patrons with access to information about community services and community calendars. As more social service agencies create their own web presence, providing access to these agencies through links from the library's home page is a natural extension of this time-honored service. Community event calendars, with hot links to sponsors or sites for further information, are other useful services. In short, the library website can be the single most important source of information about community activities and services provided locally and regionally.

RECOGNITION

Recognition of donors, supporters, and employees has long been a mainstay of library public relations. With the advent of library websites, this recognition effort has moved into new territory. The University of Pennsylvania Library's website is a prime example of the types of recognition that may be available through this medium. Links to donor websites, pictures and biographical sketches, and countless other bits of information can be linked to a description of the honoree. Of these, links to corporate donor websites can be the greatest asset. Naturally, donors enjoy seeing their names and faces in print and on the Internet, but these links can also provide tangible benefits to the donor. When shown such a link at the University of Great Falls Library website, one major donor said he could not begin to calculate the benefit his company would derive from such notice. By providing a direct link to that donor's website, the library provided well-deserved recognition for the donation and added value for the donor. While recognition is always necessary and appreciated, this added step has created new incentives for potential donors. Sample web pages that provide data on a library's supporters and recognition of its donors are shown in figures 4.3 and 4.4, respectively. For further in-depth information, consult the book *Fundraising and Friend-Raising on the Web,* by Adam Corson-Finnerty and Laura Blanchard.

Employee recognition is another area to be considered. As an extension of employee recognition programs, a library's website can provide an additional format for honoring employees. One caveat to this type of program is employee security. As Corson-Finnerty and Blanchard recommend, securing an employee's permission prior to putting names or pictures on the Web is highly recommended.

EXHIBITS

A major thrust of public relations revolves around the library's exhibits program. Libraries often invest many hours of staff time and large sums of money creating and publicizing exhibits. These productions may feature portions of the local collection, historical events, outstanding people, or traveling exhibits. The traditional exhibit usually lasts for a specific period of time and can only be viewed in person. Through

FIGURE 4.3

Sample of a Page for Library Supporters

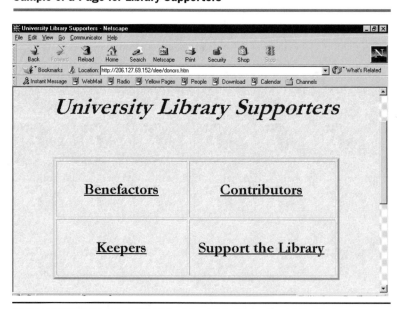

Sample created by Susan Lee, University of Great Falls Library, Great Falls, Montana. Used by permission.

the use of the Web, however, the exhibit can be viewed globally for any length of time. There are many institutions creating web-based exhibits. These include the Smithsonian Institution and the Special Collections Division of the Tulane University Library. The webography at the end of this chapter lists some of the sites this author has found. Chapter 5 contains a more detailed discussion of electronic exhibits.

GENERAL WEB DESIGN

There are many applications for web-based public relations in a library setting. What to include in any given website and, conversely, what not to include must be a local decision. However, some simple guidelines can be followed. Questions that should be answered include:

> What is the purpose of the information?
>
> Who is the intended audience?
>
> Will the library create a paper version of the information to distribute to patrons?
>
> How much time and effort will be needed to maintain this information?
>
> Is there an easier, more cost-effective means of transmitting this information to the desired audience?
>
> Does the library have the personnel, software, and equipment necessary to do an adequate job or will the work need to be outsourced?
>
> Who will maintain the website to keep it current and relevant?
>
> What training will be required for this person?

FIGURE 4.4
Sample of a Donor Recognition Page

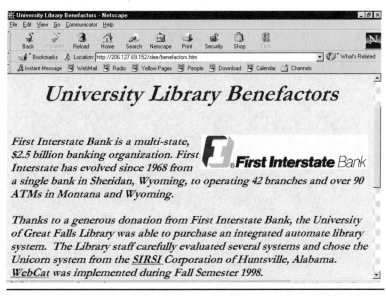

Sample created by Susan Lee, University of Great Falls Library, Great Falls, Montana.
Used by permission.

What are the long-term ramifications of creating and maintaining a library's web presence?

How will the website impact the library's existing services and programs?

The answers to these questions will provide any library administration with the basic information needed prior to jumping onto the World Wide Web bandwagon. Careful planning will allow the library to position itself in preparation for this effort. The actual mechanics of creating the library's website have been made easier through the creation of many HTML editorial software packages now available. One simply needs to develop a concept of design and then execute it using the software of choice.

A short period of time spent surfing the Web will provide many sources of design inspiration. Sites developed by large universities, nonprofit organizations, and major corporations give ample evidence of the range of possibilities that are available in web design. However, for the novice designer, the adage "Keep It Simple" is usually the best. Simplicity in design is not only easier to produce, but is often advantageous to the library's mission and purpose. The more complex the page and the more images and graphics a web page contains, the longer it will take for a potential patron to open and download the page. A common error in beginning design is to forget that many patrons may not have the high-speed connections which are usually available at the library. If the delay is too long, the patron will give up and not use the site. Also, people who are visually impaired will have difficulty reading complicated pages with complex images and graphics. This defeats the entire purpose of having the page as a communication tool. As the person responsible for creating and maintaining the library's web presence gains experience and confidence, more complex features may be added to the site.

The steps to take, then, in creating a web presence for the library include:

Focus on the target audience; know who they are.

Select specific information to be placed on the website.

Browse other library websites for additional ideas.

Select an HTML editorial software package and learn how to use it.

Obtain a website through an Internet service provider (this may be the library's parent institution).

Select an overall design style and remain consistent throughout.

Begin creating web pages—start with simple textual information and later add graphics, images, and tables.

Ask a trusted, non-librarian friend to review the website and check for the use of library lingo, overuse of acronyms, and missing information, as well as evaluate the site's general appeal.

Join the world of webmasters.

CONCLUSION

The World Wide Web offers many new possibilities for libraries. The Internet has opened new doors for libraries to allow patrons access to information about the library and its services, collections, and programs. This technology provides a new platform for old issues by providing access to the widest possible audience for materials and information available through the library. The library's public relations program can offer a new point of contact for patrons from around the corner or around the world. The Web is a new tool in the portfolio of the public relations team to provide awareness, access, outreach, recognition, and exhibits to a global market. It expands the scope of these traditional programs to potential patrons anywhere in the world with the click of a mouse.

NOTE

1. William Buchanan, introduction to *Part-Time Public Relations with Full-Time Results,* ed. Rashelle S. Karp (Chicago: American Library Association, 1995), ix.

WEBOGRAPHY

Countless numbers of excellent websites have been created in the United States. The following list of sites highlights some of the best at illustrating the various points made in this chapter.

Awareness

www.ala.org/washoff—ALA Washington Office site.

www.ala.org/pio/presskits—ALA Public Information Office press kits.

www.aclu.org—American Civil Liberties Union site.

www.amnesty.org—Amnesty International site.

Outreach/Public Calendars

www.city-of-great-falls.com—Great Falls, Montana, city site.

www.chipublib.org—Chicago Public Library site.

Recognition

www.library.upenn.edu/friends/donor.html—University of Pennsylvania Library donor recognition page.

www.lib.usf.edu/development/benefact.html—University of South Florida Library donor recognition page.

http://206.127.69.152/slee/donors.htm—University of Great Falls Library donor recognition page.

Exhibits

http://2k.si.edu—Smithsonian Institution Virtual Museum.

www.tulane.edu/~lmiller/raeburn/rivboatintro.htm—Tulane University Library On-Line Exhibit on Riverboat Jazz.

www.library.yale.edu/mssa.home1.htm—Yale University Library Manuscripts and Archives.

www.museum.olympic.org—International Olympic Museum.

Quality Sites

www.corpsofdiscovery.org—Lewis and Clark Interpretive Center, Great Falls, Montana.

www.redcross.org—American Red Cross.

SOURCES OF ADDITIONAL INFORMATION

Many books and articles have been written on using the Web for public relations. A representative list is given here.

Abels, Eileen G., Marilyn Domas White, and Karla L. Hahn. "A User-Based Design Process for Web Sites: Phase II of a Project on Design Criteria in Web Sites." *OCLC Systems & Services* 15, no. 1 (1999): 35–44.

Balas, Janet. "Doing It Right: Web Design for Library Types. Web Sites on Web Page Design." *Computers in Libraries* 20, no. 1 (January 2000): 56ff.

———. "The Don'ts of Web Page Design. Directory of Web Sites." *Computers in Libraries* 19, no. 8 (September 1999): 46–48.

———. "Using the Web to Market the Library Sites on Web Design and Promotion." *Computers in Libraries* 18, no. 8 (September 1998): 46ff.

Boudreau, Andre. "Developing Web Pages: Points to Consider." *Multimedia Information and Technology* 24, no. 4 (November 1998): 263–67.

Burgstahler, Sheryl, Dan Comden, and Beth Mabel Fraser. "Universal Access: Designing and Evaluating Web Sites for Accessibility." *Choice* 34, supp. (1997): 19–22.

Carpenter, Beth. "Your Attention, Please! Marketing Today's Libraries Using the Internet and Library Web Sites to Promote New Technology." *Computers in Libraries* 18, no. 8 (September 1998): 62–66.

Colby, Sandy. "Web Design: Creating Pearls in the Midst of Internet Sandstorms." *LLA Bulletin* 61, no. 3 (winter 1999): 156–61.

Coombs, Merolyn. "Web Site Design for Public Libraries: A Marketing Tool for the New Millennium." *Australian Library Journal* 48, no. 2 (May 1999): 117–27.

Corson-Finnerty, Adam, and Laura Blanchard. *Fundraising and Friend-Raising on the Web.* Chicago: American Library Association, 1998.

Cunningham, James L. "Ten Ways to Improve Your Web Site: Take Time to Dust Off Those Web Sites." *College & Research Libraries News* 60, no. 8 (September 1999): 614–15ff.

D'Angelo, John, and Sherry K. Little. "Successful Web Pages: What Are They and Do They Exist?" *Information Technology and Libraries* 17, no. 2 (June 1998): 71–81.

Falk, Howard. "Library Web Site Innovations in Public Libraries." *Electronic Library* 17, no. 5 (October 1999): 323–28.

Fourie, Ina. "Creating Web Sites in a Library and Information Service Environment: Some Basic Guidelines." *Mousaion* 17, no. 2 (1999): 93–113.

Garlock, Kristen L., and Sherry Piontek. *Designing Web Interfaces to Library Services and Resources.* Chicago: American Library Association, 1999.

Goudsward, David R. "Designing a Library Web Page at Dauphin County Library System." *Library Mosaics* 8 (May/June 1997): 17.

Guenther, Kim. "Publicity through Better Web Site Design." *Computers in Libraries* 19, no. 8 (September 1999): 62–64ff.

Holtz, Shel. *Public Relations on the Net: Winning Strategies to Inform and Influence the Media, the Investment Community, the Government, the Public, and More!* Boulder, Colo.: NetLibrary, 1999.

Interactive Librarian: Print and Electronic Design Techniques. Harrisburg, Pa.: Medigraphics, 2000. (A bimonthly periodical on desktop and website publishing.)

Kelly, Brian. "Web Focus: Using the Web to Promote Your Web Site." *Ariadne* (online), no. 22 (December 1999). Retrieved on August 18, 2000, from the World Wide Web at http://www.ariadne.ac.uk/issue22/web-focus.

Kent, Peter. *Poor Richard's Web Site: Geek-Free Common-Sense Advice on Building Your Own Web Site.* Denver: Top Floor, 2000.

Kim, Amy Jo. *Community Building on the Web.* Berkeley, Calif.: Peachpit, 2000.

Kohl, Susan. *Getting Attention: Leading-Edge Lessons for Publicity and Marketing.* Boston: Butterworth-Heinemann, 2000.

LaSalle, Kim. *Life in Cyberspace: Internet, Public Relations and Marketing.* Indianapolis: LaSalle Communications, 1995.

Linden, Julie. "The Library's Web Site Is the Library: Designing for Distance Learners." *College & Research Libraries News* 61, no. 2 (February 2000): 99, 101.

Medeiros, Norm. "Academic Library Web Sites: From Public Relations to Information Gateway." *College & Research Libraries News* 60, no. 7 (July/August 1999): 527–29ff.

Middleton, Iain, Michael McConnell, and Grant Davidson. "Presenting a Model for the Structure and Content of a University World Wide Web Site." *Journal of Information Science* 25, no. 3 (1999): 219–27.

Nicotera, Cynthia L. "Information Access by Design: Electronic Guidelines for Librarians, Designing Web Pages." *Information Technology and Libraries* 18, no. 2 (June 1999): 104–8.

Quint, Barbara E. "Designing the Perfect Information Portal." *Information Today* 17, no. 2 (February 2000): 7–8, 10.

Regel, Jennifer. "The Internet and Public Relations Tips for Library Web Sites." *Mississippi Libraries* 60 (winter 1996): 99–100.

Renton, Nicholas Edwin. *Public Relations, Newsletters and Internet Usage for Organisations.* East Roseville, N.S.W., Australia: Kangaroo, 1997.

Sherwin, Gregory R., and Emily N. Avila. *Connecting Online: Creating a Successful Image on the Internet.* Grants Pass, Ore.: Oasis, 1997.

Witmer, Diane F. *Spinning the Web: A Handbook for Public Relations on the Internet.* New York: Longman, 2000.

Exhibits

DOROTHY CHRISTIANSEN AND CHANDLER JACKSON

An exhibits program can provide visitors to the library a sense of what the library is, what the strengths of its collection are, and a general feel for the interests of those who use the library. Whether the exhibit is a traditional display of materials and artifacts in cases in the building or a virtual exhibit of similar objects, an exhibit program can be an effective means of communicating with the library's visitors.

WHAT ARE EXHIBITS?

Exhibits are displays, physical or virtual, of items that increase a library's visibility and inform library users about a library's collections and services. An exhibits program includes all of the steps that go into creating an exhibit or group of exhibits. This type of program provides opportunities for a library to develop partnerships with its communities, thereby increasing a library's base of local support and making people more aware of the library.

CREATING AN EXHIBITS PROGRAM

Most aspects of creating an exhibits program are the same whether the exhibit is a physical display in the library or a virtual display viewable through the World Wide Web. Unless stated to the contrary, each of the following steps pertains to all types and formats of exhibits.

In order to mount a successful exhibits program, the following steps should be taken.

STEP ONE
Put Someone in Charge

A successful exhibits program will ideally be managed from start to finish by the same person or group of people. This will help to ensure that exhibits and displays consistently meet standards for quality, and it will help to avoid confusion when an external group requests space in the library for an exhibit. Most libraries contemplating a virtual exhibit will assign someone with technical expertise to assist the exhibits coordinator with technical decisions necessary for mounting a virtual exhibit. However, the exhibits coordinator is still the person responsible for the overall direction of the program.

STEP TWO
Develop an Exhibits Program Policy

An exhibits program policy (see figure 5.1) is an official statement which (1) identifies the types of exhibits that can be mounted in the library and on the library's website; (2) indicates how individuals or groups can apply to use exhibit space; and (3) provides criteria that will be used to approve or reject an exhibit application.

The parts of an exhibit program policy usually include the following sections:

Goals and Objectives

This section describes the goals and objectives for the exhibits program. Specifically, what does the organization hope to achieve from the exhibits program? Why is it important for the library to have an exhibits program? What, in the end, are the benefits?

Exhibits Coordinator

This part of the policy identifies the staff who will be responsible for the program. It also identifies their responsibilities.

Criteria

This portion of the policy defines who can mount exhibits in library exhibit space, for what purpose, and how the exhibit materials should be presented. It also describes the criteria that are used to accept or reject an exhibit application.

Procedures

This portion of the exhibits policy:

> Informs all potential exhibitors of the procedures involved in applying for exhibit space. Exhibit applications (see figure 5.2) should supply information regarding the nature and purpose of the exhibit, when the exhibit is to be mounted, how long it will be left up, and where it should be placed in the library.
>
> Describes the review process by which applications are accepted or rejected.
>
> Indicates the types of insurance and security that the library will provide for exhibits.
>
> Outlines any procedures necessary for the circulation of exhibited materials.

FIGURE 5.1
Library Exhibits Policy

EXHIBITS POLICY
Wonderful Public Library

The library makes exhibit cases and other display areas, including space on the library website, available for display of materials which support the institution's programs and services. Of special interest to the library are exhibits that promote the library's collections, services, and programs, or relate to the local community. Exhibits should contribute positively to the library's environment, highlight collection strengths, publicize the resources and services of the library, enrich the life of the community, and be a means of strengthening partnerships between the library and its community.

EXHIBITS COORDINATOR

The Exhibits Coordinator is responsible for exhibits mounted in the library or on the library's website.

The responsibilities of the Exhibits Coordinator are:

To develop and execute an annual plan of exhibits

To review incoming requests for mounting an exhibit

To mount exhibits

To assist exhibitors who wish to mount exhibits

CRITERIA FOR EXHIBITS

Exhibits accepted for display in the library's exhibit and display areas should satisfy the following criteria:

Relate to the mission of the library and its parent organization

Be sponsored by the library or an approved individual, organization, or agency

Be fair and equitable concerning issues of potential controversy

Be aesthetically pleasing

Display materials relevant to the theme of the exhibit

Promote the materials, services, and functions of the library or resources in the local community

Facilitate cooperative relations between the library and the community it serves

PROCEDURES

An application form should be obtained from the Exhibits Coordinator or the library's administrative office. The form should be submitted at least three months in advance of the proposed date of the requested exhibit.

The application form should be returned to the Exhibits Coordinator or the library's administrative office. If delivered to the office, it will be forwarded to the Exhibits Coordinator, who will respond to the person requesting permission to mount an exhibit.

The Exhibits Coordinator will review all applications and make a decision to approve or reject the application.

The Exhibits Coordinator will assess all applications on the basis of the criteria listed above. Applicants will be informed, by the Exhibits Coordinator, of the status (approval/rejection) of their applications. Successful applicants will be provided with a confirmed time and place for the proposed exhibit.

Exhibits must be ready for installation and must include all necessary identifying labels. Unless otherwise indicated, it is the responsibility of the exhibitor to dismantle the exhibit after the display period is completed.

Insurance for items of value used in exhibits and not owned by the library is the responsibility of the donor of the item(s).

Circulation of items: All items owned by the library and borrowed from library collections for display purposes must be charged out to EXHIBIT according to established procedures. Items on exhibit are subject to recall compliance.

FIGURE 5.2
Application for Exhibit/Display Space

APPLICATION FOR EXHIBIT/DISPLAY SPACE

Name:_____

Address:_____

_____

Department/Organization: _____

Telephone Number: _____

Proposed Dates for Exhibit: _____

Proposed Title of Exhibit: _____

Please describe the purpose and nature of the exhibit, relating the description to the attached Exhibits Policy (attach to this form).

Cases/Space requested—list preference:

	LOCATION	SIZE
_____	Library Lobby	72″ × 36″ × 9″ flat (2 cases)
_____	Library Lobby	60″ × 22″ × 9″ flat (4 cases)
_____	Library Lower Level	72″ × 45″ × 18″ upright (2 cases, 4 glass shelves per case)
_____	Virtual Exhibit	
_____	Space, No cases	Area Size _____
_____	Computer/Server Space	Megabyte Size of Exhibit _____

Signature_____   Date _____

Please return application form to: Exhibits Coordinator, Address, Telephone number,
E-mail, Fax number

This area is for use by the Exhibits Coordinator.

Decision or Recommendation of the Exhibits Coordinator:

Signature_____   Date _____

STEP THREE
Identify Space, Equipment, Supplies, and Budgetary Needs

Space

Exhibits must be able to be seen by the users. For example, exhibit cases and bulletin boards should be located in primary traffic areas but should not interfere with the traffic flow. Virtual exhibits must be linked from a primary page within the website.

Informational signs must be placed at strategic locations to inform library users about exhibits at the library.

Equipment

Choose the medium for the exhibit carefully. Library supply catalogs and furniture catalogs advertise many types of exhibit cases (ranging from flat glass cases to upright shelved units) and bulletin boards (wall-mounted units to movable display panels). The choice of an exhibit case or bulletin board should be determined by (1) the available space, (2) the type of exhibit, (3) preservation considerations, (4) the budget, and (5) security (for example, lockable cases and bulletin boards are essential in unsupervised areas).

Obtain access to a microcomputer and laser printer with appropriate software for printing signs and text. The computer must also have the capability of producing web pages for virtual exhibits.

Supplies

Exhibit supplies include everything from basic office supplies (such as scissors, staplers, scotch tape, thumbtacks, rulers, colored paper, colored markers, and rubber cement) to "exhibit-specific" supplies such as book display stands, blocks to vary the height of displayed items, lettering templates, colored poster board, ultraviolet plexiglass to protect displayed items, and colored background cloth.

In many instances, exhibit supplies are reusable (display stands, thumbtacks), and in some instances, the supplies that are available determine the type of exhibit to be mounted.

Budget

Other than staff time, the most costly part of an exhibits program is the one-time purchase of display cases, wall-mounted units, and computer equipment/software.

An annual exhibits program budget should include exhibit supplies and, if traveling exhibits are going to be used, transportation, shipping, and other related costs. The cost of insuring exhibit materials must also be factored into the budget, unless the library's general liability policy covers these items.

STEP FOUR
Develop Security, Preservation, and Circulation Strategies

Security Strategies

Although a library's exhibit policy will ideally place insurance responsibility for loaned items on the loaner, materials on exhibit (including library exhibits, loaned exhibits, and traveling exhibits) must be protected from loss or vandalism. Whenever possible, exhibits should be displayed in locked exhibit or wall cases and bulletin boards.

Preservation Strategies

Librarians must take extreme care not to display materials in ways which are harmful to them. For example, if the exhibit is to be up for an extended period or if it includes manuscripts or rare materials, temperature and humidity should be monitored at all times and ultraviolet plexiglass should be used to protect the items from ultraviolet rays. Librarians should avoid placing exhibit cases in direct sunlight, since sunlight fades documents and heat speeds deterioration. Finally, in order to avoid chemical reactions between display items and their mounting apparatus, librarians should use inert materials such as plexiglass, acrylic, and covered metal, rather than wood.

Circulation Strategies

The best evidence that an exhibits program is working might be when patrons ask to borrow books that are in the exhibit. The library's general circulation policy should include policies and procedures for the circulation of exhibit materials. Generally, a more liberal circulation policy is desirable, since the purpose of many exhibits is to increase circulation. Sometimes it is better to loan an item from an exhibit, even if the loan results in a less aesthetically pleasing display. Often, librarians purchase duplicate copies of items on display so that the second copy can be circulated while the first copy is unavailable. Reserve lists for items can also be used after the exhibit is over.

STEP FIVE
Prepare a Schedule and Develop Presentation Guidelines

Planning effective exhibits requires consideration of community and institutional calendars in order to avoid conflicts in the scheduling of events such as a kickoff for the exhibit, or special events which utilize the exhibit. An exhibit must also be planned far enough in advance so that sufficient preparation time is allotted.

The following recommendations should be considered in designing a physical exhibit.

The choice of a type of case for an exhibit depends upon the types of materials that are to be included. For example, books and artifacts are best presented in locked upright shelved cases or in flat cases. In contrast, two-dimensional materials such as posters, pictures, and brochures are best presented on bulletin boards and panel boards.

The individuals who prepared an exhibit should always be acknowledged somewhere in the exhibit. In some instances, an exhibit guide, explanatory flier, brochure, or a selected reading list can be made available near the exhibit.

All exhibits must have a clearly stated theme or focus which is made known to viewers by a title label or a title label with a paragraph of explanation.

Display materials must be directly related to the stated theme of an exhibit.

The style and arrangement of materials throughout all the cases of an exhibit should be consistent.

Hardware (book racks and plastic elevators) should be consistent throughout an exhibit, and should be as invisible as possible to the viewer.

Layout of exhibits should be simple in order not to draw attention away from exhibited items.

One typeface style should be used for all of the labels in an exhibit. Twelve-point typeface for text, and 14- to 16-point typeface for exhibit titles are recommended. In order to emphasize text within labels (e.g., a book title or an interesting quote), different styles within a typeface can be used (e.g., bold or italics).

Labels should be mounted on acid-free mat board backing (one subtle color should be used throughout the exhibit) to prevent them from curling.

Labels should be provided for each item or group of similar items to explain how they fit into the theme of the exhibit. If the exhibited item is a book and the author/title is not visible to the viewer, the author and title should be cited on a label. If the exhibit carries over into non-contiguous cases (e.g., first floor and reserve area), a label in the last contiguous case should direct viewers to the next case.

The amount of text on each label should be consistent throughout the exhibit. As a rule of thumb, one to two lines fit comfortably on a 5" $\times$ 2" label; one to two paragraphs fit on a 5"$\times$ 5" or 7" $\times$ 10" label.

To hold a book open to a particular page without impeding the visibility of the text or damaging the book, use clear mylar tape. To highlight text from a book without damaging the book, use clear yellow cellophane, trimmed to fit the size of the text to be highlighted and then laid over the text. Another way to highlight text is to cut out small colored arrows (complementary to the color of the label's background board) and lay them next to the text to be highlighted. Never use highlighter pens.

Cases should not be overly full.

The following recommendations should be considered in designing a virtual exhibit.

Control technology—don't let the technology control you. Design the exhibit to utilize the available technology but remember that variations exist in the capabilities of browsers. Whenever possible, view the exhibit using different browsers and monitor sizes to see the differences in the impact and appearance of the exhibit prior to release.

Communicate the message immediately. Seventy percent of the viewers will only see the first page.

Create the design elements with download time in mind—tables and colors do not add to the download time, but other design features might. Gimmicks tend to detract from the message of the exhibit.

Size of image is important because it affects the download time of a web page. Thumbnail images are a convenient means of providing the viewer with a quick-loading example of the image that can be linked to a larger image file for more detailed viewing.

Labeling information is as important in a virtual exhibit as in a physical display. Linking the textual information to the image is important. This can be done in many ways, including placing the textual material on the page with the thumbnail image or on a separate page with a hot link imbedded in the title of the image. Directions for accessing such information should be included with the image.

STEP SIX
Prepare Publicity

Once the exhibit is planned, a news release about the exhibit should be sent to a variety of media (chapter 2 in this book provides guidelines on preparing and distributing news releases). If possible, the release should be sent at least two to four weeks in advance of the exhibit opening. And after the exhibit opens, a photo can be sent with an additional news release in which the ongoing success of the exhibit is detailed.

STEP SEVEN
Evaluate the Exhibits Program

Evaluation should examine the entire exhibits program, as well as the individual exhibits and displays that make up the program. Questions that might be asked include:

Are the exhibits/displays meeting the criteria set forth in the exhibits policy?

Is the informal (word of mouth) feedback about the exhibits positive?

Are additional suggestions for other exhibits being received?

Are any of the exhibits being picked up by the local media for a news article or broadcast comments?

In what ways can the program be improved?

Is it worth having an exhibits/display program?

To get answers to these questions, librarians must be vigilant. It helps to have a notebook where comments are recorded, and, if time and staff are available, a short survey can be handed out to people after they have viewed the exhibit. A link to the e-mail of the exhibits coordinator with an invitation for comments can achieve similar results for a virtual exhibit.

SOURCES OF ADDITIONAL INFORMATION

Barteluk, Wendy D. M. *Library Displays on a Shoestring: Three-Dimensional Techniques for Promoting Library Services*. Metuchen, N.J.: Scarecrow, 1993.

Borgwardt, Stephanie. *Library Display*. 2nd ed. Johannesburg: Witwatersrand University Press, 1970.

Casterline, Gail Farr. *Archives and Manuscripts: Exhibits*. Chicago: Society of American Archivists, 1980.

Coplan, Kate. *Effective Library Exhibits: How to Prepare and Promote Good Displays.* 2nd ed. Dobbs Ferry, N.Y.: Oceana, 1974.

Dubber, Elizabeth, et al. *Displays and Publicity for the School Library.* Swindon, U.K.: School Library Association, 1996.

Evans, Earlene Green, and Muriel Miller Branch. *3-D Displays for Libraries, Schools, and Media Centers.* Jefferson, N.C.: McFarland, 2000.

Everhart, Nancy, Claire Hartz, and William Kreiger. *Library Displays.* Metuchen, N.J.: Scarecrow, 1989.

Garvey, Mona. *Library Displays: Their Purpose, Construction and Use.* New York: H. W. Wilson, 1969.

Kemp, Jane, et al. *Displays and Exhibits in College Libraries.* Chicago: Association of College and Research Libraries, 1997.

Kohn, Rita. *Experiencing Displays.* Metuchen, N.J.: Scarecrow, 1982.

Schaeffer, Mark. *Library Displays Handbook.* New York: H. W. Wilson, 1991.

Serrell, Beverly. *Exhibit Labels: An Interpretive Approach.* Lanham, Md.: Alta Mira, 1996.

Tedeschi, Anne C. *Book Displays: A Library Exhibits Handbook.* Fort Atkinson, Wis.: Highsmith, 1997.

Whole Person Catalog. Chicago: American Library Association, n.d.

WEBOGRAPHY: QUALITY VIRTUAL EXHIBITS

http://2k.si.edu—This is the site of the Virtual Smithsonian. A very large exhibit, this shows what can exist in the virtual world.

http://www.christusrex.org/www1/vaticano/0-musei.html—An exhibit of the treasures of the Vatican Museum.

http://www.dm-art.org/permcoll_home.htm—The Dallas Museum of Art provides another style of presenting a virtual exhibit.

http://www.nara.gov/exhall/—The site of the National Archives and Records Administration online exhibit is an example of another method of displaying artifacts and the accompanying information.

http://sil.si.edu/silpublications/online-exhibitions/—This site features links to online exhibitions created by libraries, archives, and historical societies, as well as to museum online exhibitions that focus on library and archival materials (such as printed books, book illustrations, manuscripts, photographs, printed ephemera, posters, archival audio and video recordings, artists' books, and the book arts). The site includes a separate introduction. The list of exhibitions is arranged alphabetically by title and shows the names of the sponsoring institutions.

http://www.tulane.edu/~lmiller/carnival.html—This exhibit of the Tulane University collection of materials related to Mardi Gras shows how other information about the library might be displayed along with the exhibit. This feature allows the virtual visitor, who has been attracted by the exhibit, the opportunity to visit other features of the library and its services.

ORGANIZATIONS TO CONTACT FOR MORE INFORMATION

ALA Graphics
American Library Association
50 East Huron St.
Chicago, IL 60611
http://alastore.ala.org

Exhibition Catalog Awards Committee
Rare Books and Manuscripts Section
Association of College and Research
    Libraries
American Library Association
http://www.rbms.nd.edu/#exhibition

Exhibits Round Table (ERT)
American Library Association
http://www.ala.org/alaort/rtables/ert

Exhibits Task Force
Map and Geography Round Table
American Library Association
http://www.uni.edu/moore/magrost.html

Public Information Office
American Library Association
http://www.ala.org/pio/

Traveling Exhibitions Program
Interpretive Programs Office
Library of Congress. Contact the Senior
    Exhibits Director
    (202-707-5223).
http://lcweb.loc.gov/exhibits

Traveling Exhibitions Program
Public Programs Office
American Library Association
http://www.ala.org/publicprograms/
    travel.html

Interactive Multimedia Programs via Touch Screen Kiosks and CD-ROMs

SUSAN M. HILTON

Interactive multimedia programs can provide a fascinating and engaging way for library patrons and potential visitors to gather information. These programs can be delivered via a touch screen kiosk either inside or outside of the library, or on a CD-ROM that can be distributed to patrons in any number of ways. These programs use traditional text and graphics, along with audio, video, and animated materials that give library programs and information an active and dynamic appearance. The creation of such programs can be challenging, difficult, time-consuming, and expensive, but often the benefits of such a program are worth the effort. And once the software used to create them is learned, updating the program on a regular basis, or expanding it, can be quick and painless.

BENEFITS OF TOUCH SCREEN KIOSKS AND CD-ROMS

The primary benefit of providing information and announcements to visitors through a touch screen kiosk or a CD-ROM is that these media attract positive attention. The impression that is created is one of a modern, technologically able institution that uses cutting-edge information delivery systems. Other benefits are summarized below.

> Kiosks offer visitors an interactive experience and the chance to explore the library and its attendant exhibits, displays, and programs as their interests dictate.

> Kiosks can be designed to fit nicely into environments that vary from traditional to modern.

> Kiosk information is readily available 24 hours a day without the need for a staff person at an information desk.

> Library patrons who are uncomfortable asking for help from a person are now able to get the answers to questions without embarrassment.

> Young people and children are especially attracted to touch screen programs and may spend more time exploring information that is pre-

sented on a touch screen than they would using traditional information delivery vehicles.

The program that is housed in the computer can also be downloaded or transferred to CD-ROM form, allowing library staff to send the CDs to interested people, organizations, or institutions.

Advancing technology and falling costs have placed CD-ROM creation within the financial and technical reach of the average library organization.

Updating a kiosk program on a regular basis ensures that the kiosk's information is current and timely, and keeping new and fresh information on the kiosk encourages regular visitors to continue to use the kiosk. Once the software is learned, making corrections, changes, or additions can be quick and painless.

APPLICATIONS

Touch screen kiosks can provide an array of information to library visitors at the touch of a finger. Standard topics include guides to the library, lists of services that are regularly provided, schedules of events and activities, staff directories that highlight credentials and areas of expertise, promotions for library-related organizations, and fundraising and donations options to which the visitor might contribute. The extent to which materials are placed in this form can be determined by the time and expertise available, the computing skills of the staff, and the funding sources. Once a kiosk is in place, the programs it contains can be expanded or contracted based on the needs and interests of the patrons.

DESIGN PROCEDURES

There are several aspects of the design process for interactive multimedia that distinguish it from designing in other media. These are to:

determine which of the various media choices will best deliver the content;

provide an effective screen design that is both attractive and easy to use; and

connect the various branches of the program in a way that allows users to move easily from place to place as they readily locate the information they seek.

Determine Which of the Various Media Choices
Will Best Deliver the Content

Matching media with content is always an important step in design. In multimedia, the designer can use text, graphics, audio, video, and animation. And equally important, each user will be able to find a match for his or her preferred method of learning. However, opportunities for redundancy can be both a help and a hindrance. One way to avoid overdoing the repetition of information is to build in provisions for users to select the medium they desire. For instance, a user may choose to play an audio message that repeats in some form the text or graphic information on the screen, or she may choose to turn the audio message off.

Provide an Effective Screen Design That Is Both Attractive and Easy to Use

Selecting an appropriate screen design is both challenging and fun. Interface options include metaphors such as a physical space, a book or other object that is familiar to library visitors, or an anthropomorphic guide or host. Successful programs have also been created using the library building as the design metaphor, with a cartoon-type character as a guide or host. Other programs set up material in chapters or various volumes within a set.

Figure 6.1 is a sample of a screen design using an illustrated map of a museum grounds as a menu. The items outlined in white are "hot" and will respond to a mouse click (or touch in this case) by moving to a new section in the program. For instance, touching the museum building will take the user to a section featuring the exhibits found inside the building. Touching the oil derrick will open a section about oil-drilling history and the oil-producing region. When the program is displayed on a touch screen monitor, information about each section is displayed near the icon to provide the user with a guide.

FIGURE 6.1
Example of a Screen Design

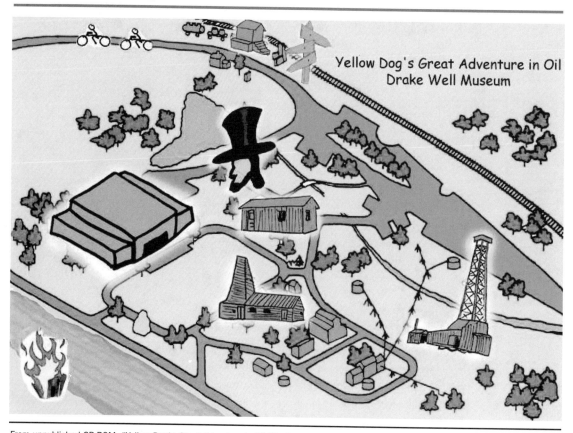

Yellow Dog's Great Adventure in Oil
Drake Well Museum

From unpublished CD-ROM, "Yellow Dog's Great Adventure in Oil," by Drake Well Park. Used with permission.

Connect the Various Branches of the Program in a Way That Allows Users to Move Easily from Place to Place As They Readily Locate the Information They Seek

In addition to a pleasing design, the creator must consider the usability of the program. Patrons approaching the kiosk must be able to learn quickly how to interact with the screen. Tools must be available, easily identifiable, and consistently placed. From screen to screen, users should find navigation tools in the same place at the same time. Provisions should also be made for the user to jump from one branch to another. For instance, in a section about calendar events, a user might want to explore library holdings related to a speaker series, or learn more about the presenters or staff in charge of an event. The designer should anticipate the desires of users, if possible, and decide to what extent the program can accommodate such movement. High interactivity and a great deal of navigation are useful to patrons but are more challenging for the designer. He or she should make decisions based on a good balance between the two extremes.

In figure 6.2, a screen provides information about the items to be found on the museum grounds. On the right side of the screen are the navigation tools the viewer has learned to use and that are present throughout the program. The derrick returns the user to the main menu of the program, and the oil splat is the exit. Also present on this screen is Yellow Dog, the animated host of the program. This character is based on the yellow dog lantern that was used during the early days of oil drilling, and serves as a narrator and host throughout the program.

FIGURE 6.2
Examples of Navigation Tools

Did you know that you could move drilling rigs from place to place? Some were pulled by horses, and others were driven on the backs of trucks. You could DRIVE to your oil well site, and drill for oil from your truck!

In the Transportation Building at Drake Well Park, you can see some of these trucks, and find out all of the ways that oil has been moved from place to place.

From unpublished CD-ROM, "Yellow Dog's Great Adventure in Oil," by Drake Well Park. Used with permission.

SOFTWARE

There are several software programs available that make designing and producing interactive multimedia programs a reasonable goal for the average layperson. A good way to evaluate multimedia authoring programs is to ask other software users who have produced multimedia programs for advice. Software producers are usually willing to talk about what works—and what doesn't. Software users should pay special attention to the level of expertise required before choosing a particular multimedia software program. While programs that provide many features and have powerful creative capabilities may seem desirable, awareness of one's own computer abilities and those of the staff who must maintain the program should be considered. Better a simple but well-designed and attractive program than a killer of a program that doesn't run. The programs described below are only a short list of the possible software programs one might use.[1]

Macromedia Authorware 5.1

This program uses a complex set of icons to allow the designer to create screens and interaction. While it is difficult initially, it offers the designer a huge number of ways for users to interact with the computer. Designers should use this program if their goal is to allow the user opportunities to answer questions, take quizzes, or enter plenty of data through the keyboard. This program also offers publishing to CD, DVD, and on the Web. The program can be purchased for a Macintosh or Windows-based computer, and is by far the most complex of the programs on this list. Potential purchasers can visit www.macromedia.com on the Internet for more information about this software. (Macromedia, Inc. Cost: $2,713.99.)

Toolbook II Instructor

This Windows-only program uses the book metaphor, allowing the creator to design programs as they would appear on the printed page. It is easy to use and offers many advanced features, including the ability to track the user's movements and responses. It is especially good for training and instruction. Potential purchasers can visit www.click2learn.com on the Internet for more information. (Click2Learn. Cost: $995.)

Macromedia Director 8 Shockwave Studio

This program allows the user to create "movies" by arranging multimedia elements on a timeline, providing for their presence on the screen. It is fairly easy to use and doesn't require much programming knowledge, but it still allows for lots of navigation and interaction. It also allows programs to be created for the Web or other media and is available in both Macintosh and Windows versions. To learn more about this program, visit www.macromedia.com on the Internet. (Macromedia, Inc. Cost: $999.)

Toolbook II Assistant

This program is an easier-to-use version of the Instructor program. It features drag and drop tools that allow designers to pull onto the screen the various elements needed. For more information, see www.click2learn.com on the Internet. (Click2Learn. Cost: $695.)

Supercard

This Macintosh-based program provides templates that allow designers to jump into production quickly. An advanced level of Mac-based authoring based on the earlier Hypercard product, Supercard produces more sophisticated programs that can link to databases. This may be useful for designers who want to provide access to the library's holdings information. More information is available at www.incwell.com on the Internet. (Incwell Technologies Digital Media Group. Cost: $144.95.)

Multimedia designers who wish to produce CD-ROMs can now purchase computers that include CD-ROM burners. The use of such technology has become easier over the past few years. In most cases, a blank CD-R costs less than one dollar, and can be purchased (usually in a 3-pack or 10-pack) at an office supply store. By placing the blank CD-R in the burner drive and following the directions that come with the CD-ROM burner software, an average computer user can produce a CD-ROM that contains a copy of a program. This can then be distributed to interested people and organizations, or can be made available in other libraries. The printed inserts in the plastic cases that hold the CD-ROM (called jewel cases) can be produced by purchasing a kit for these materials (most label companies sell these kits at office supply stores). The kit provides users with computer software and the peripherals necessary to produce the labels. The inserts in the jewel case can feature the program's title and other information on both the front and back. Producing these materials on an ink-jet printer is easy and inexpensive.

PRODUCTION TIPS

More Isn't Always More

Production of multimedia programs is exciting and fun—up to a point! It is easy to get carried away with the wide array of options available. The possibilities seem endless. This is known in the trade as "feature creep"—we could do this, and then we could do this, and oh! then we could do this! Soon the program that seemed simple in its initial concept has grown in size and scope until its completion seems far away, or unlikely altogether. While it isn't a bad thing to dream of the possibilities, remember that with every additional feature or option, the designer must commit more time, effort, and money to the final program. The best way to determine what options should or should not be added to the program is to weigh it against the initial purpose by asking, "How much does this feature enable the program to meet its intended purpose?"

Limit Video and Audio to Short Segments

Short pieces of audio and/or video can add interest and excitement to a segment that may otherwise seem dull. Certain types of content benefit from being presented through sound and/or motion. Action and music clearly aid users in understanding the message. However, these pieces eat up the computer's memory, and may cause the screen action to slow down, or stop altogether. When an audio or video message is clearly the way to go, then use it. If the use of audio or video isn't called for by the content, then it may be best to eliminate it.

Take Advantage of the Program's Nonlinear Structure

When designing the structure of a multimedia program, try to think like the potential user. What other topics, ideas, or parts of the program might the user like to see next? For example, if the program is presenting information about a visiting storyteller in the section about upcoming library programs, is it reasonable for the user to be able to click to a biography of this person, a list of books authored by her, or a short video/audio clip of the storyteller interacting with her audience? Think about what the user might like to know, and then offer reasonable possibilities (but watch out for feature creep).

Make It Easy to Update

A program that requires frequent changes and modifications can become a burden to its owner. However, any program that will offer useful information to library visitors must be updated at some regular intervals. The way to make this process less painful is to limit current information to certain screens or sections, making certain that other screens contain only generic information that doesn't require frequent updating.

LEGAL RAMIFICATIONS

Copyright Issues

The Digital Millennium Copyright Act spells out what a designer may or may not include in his program.[2] Designers must make certain that they haven't unfairly or illegally used materials that are not theirs to use.

Stock Art

If stock clip art, photos, sound files from sound libraries, or video files from stock sources are to be used, designers must make certain to read the fine print carefully. Many of the offerings are royalty-free, but some sources require varying levels of compensation, depending on the program's intended use.

Software Acknowledgment

Most of the authoring programs available require that the name or logo of the program be presented somewhere in the program. There are also licensing agreements that must be completed with the company when a production, created with their software, is made available to the public. Again, read the fine print carefully.

COST

The cost of a stand-alone touch screen kiosk can range from $4,500 to $8,000. The casing itself can vary widely in cost depending upon the material, size, color, and additional features needed. For instance, if a printer slot is included or a tray must be built in to accommodate a keyboard, the cost goes up. The author has dealt with companies that provide kiosks in two basic colors—black or white. However, any color can be provided for significant extra cost. It is usually more cost effective to use an attractive label that makes the kiosk appear to be custom-made!

Building the touch screen monitor into the wall and thus bypassing the need for a free-standing kiosk can save money and has other benefits as well. When the monitor is anchored in the wall the computer cannot be damaged or stolen, the kiosk doesn't take up valuable floor space, and the monitor can fit handsomely into an exhibit without being intrusive. However, this requires making permanent modifications to the library, and must be done in a manner that allows access to the computer and monitor. Consequently, this option involves some planning. But if renovations are being made for some other reason, it might be a good time to include a kiosk.

If the multimedia kiosk is to include a printer (to allow patrons to take away printed copy of certain information), expect to pay significantly for thermal printers. These are the types of printers one might find at a self-service gasoline pump, chosen because they are dependable and can provide clear printed material without the need for attention or maintenance. However, the cost of these features may be substantial.

Attachment to the Web is also an option that may or may not cost additional money. Often a wired facility can have a drop at the site where the kiosk will be located without much additional trouble. The ability to access the Web adds much to the usefulness of the program.

NOTES

1. Prices and versions are current as of November 2000.

2. The full text of the Digital Millennium Copyright Act can be found at the following URL: www.loc.gov/copyright/legislation/hr2281.pdf. For more information about the act and its impact on libraries, go to www.arl.org/info/frn/copy/dmca.html.

SOURCES OF ADDITIONAL INFORMATION

Extensive materials are available for those who want to learn more about interactive multimedia design and production. These books have proven useful to many beginning designers. In addition, much material is available to help the beginner learn to use software. Especially helpful in this regard is the Peachpit QuickStart Guide series, whose publications provide guidance on becoming proficient in the basics of a number of computer software packages. Each QuickStart book focuses on lessons and activities to guide the user in a specific program. The books can be ordered from Peachpit Press, 1249 Eighth Street, Berkeley, CA 94710; telephone: (510) 524-2178; fax: (510) 524-2221; www.peachpit.com. Another especially helpful resource is the Classroom in a Book series published by Adobe Press. Each book in the series provides lessons and practice activities in print and on CD for Adobe software programs. Information about the books in the series can be obtained at www. adobe.com/products/cib/main.html, and the books can be ordered through Amazon.com.

Graham, Lisa. *The Principles of Interactive Design.* Albany, N.Y.: Delmar, 1999.

Stansberry, Domenic. *Labyrinths: The Art of Interactive Writing and Design.* Belmont, Calif.: Wadsworth, 1998.

Strauss, Roy. *Managing Multimedia Projects.* Boston: Focal, 1997.

Vaughan, Tay. *Multimedia: Making It Work.* 5th ed. Berkeley, Calif.: McGraw Hill, 2001.

Planning
Special Events

DEBORA MESKAUSKAS

A special event is an event that will be held just once and is focused on a specific objective. Special events may be focused on attracting new audiences, current audiences, or both. For example, a special event might be planned to celebrate a specific chapter in an organization's development by staging a groundbreaking ceremony, building dedication, or anniversary celebration. Special events are always created for a targeted purpose and audience, and may include functions such as literary luncheons, fundraisers, job fairs, or awards banquets. It is important for event planners to note the distinction between library programs and special events. Library programs are defined as regularly scheduled, continuing offerings such as lecture series, library instruction classes, book discussion groups, story hours, and summer reading clubs. Special events are one-time events focused on a specific purpose.

CREATING A SPECIAL EVENT

The following steps will promote a successful event.

STEP ONE
Develop Strategies for Success

Determine the purpose of the event and what the library is trying to achieve by establishing specific and measurable objectives that the event is intended to accomplish. For example, is the library trying to attract non-users, unite patrons with a common interest, recognize an honoree or a volunteer group's efforts, or raise money? As objectives are being defined, make sure that the purpose of the special event is important enough to merit the time and expense that will be necessary in order to stage, publicize, and evaluate the event.

Match the type of event that is selected to the purpose it serves. Target the segments of the population that would be most receptive to this type of event. For example, a library scheduling a seminar on annuities might aim its promotion at professionals in the workforce rather than teenagers working at McDonald's. A library scheduling a Victorian tea might aim its promotion at women, especially if the event is held in early May and promoted as the perfect Mother's Day gift for mom or sweetheart.

Determine special groups that may have a stake in the event so that the special event's total attendance potential can be realized. Do not forget to include library patrons, local legislators, business and community leaders, senior citizens, students, and ethnic populations.

Ensure that the library staff fully supports the special event and that there are enough staff and volunteers for on-site management of the event.

Start the planning at least three months, and in many cases, one year, ahead of time. Be aware of community events during the event's time frame that could compete for the audience's attendance and possibly dilute the event's effectiveness.

Develop ways to evaluate the event's success. Measurable objectives might include attendance, amount of money raised, number of new library cards issued, increases in circulation of materials, or audience feedback in the form of overall perceptions or a pretest and posttest to determine if the information provided was assimilated.

If possible, talk to other librarians or examine websites from other libraries that describe successful similar events.

STEP TWO
Develop a Checklist

A checklist provides a step-by-step guide to organize and execute a special event. Figure 7.1 is an example of a checklist for an open house special event. A time line can also be incorporated into the event checklist.

STEP THREE
Create the Budget

The objective of an event budget is to provide the event planners with a financial blueprint. The budget should be specific, and it should include pre-event expenses such as printing, postage, permits, and insurance; event costs such as speakers, entertainment, food, supplies, and security; and revenue opportunities such as ticket sales, sponsorships, donations, and concession sales.

STEP FOUR
Broaden the Library's Base with Sponsors

One way to broaden an event budget is to go outside the organization to foster new relationships for funding through partnerships with local businesses. As the search for new sources of revenue gets increasingly competitive, libraries must be creative in investigating revenue-generating relationships.

FIGURE 7.1
Open House Checklist

_____ Select chair and members of the Planning Committee.

_____ Planning Committee sets event date and develops master plan for the Open House.

_____ Select chairs for each of the following subcommittees:

> _____ *Arrangement Subcommittee*
> Plans tour routes, prepares and sets up exhibits, displays, demonstrations.

> _____ *Hosts Subcommittee*
> Greets guests, handles registration, mingles with guests, distributes booklets, annual reports, and other related literature as guests arrive and leave.

> _____ *Tour Guides Subcommittee* (One member for every ten guests)
> Conducts tours, answers questions, keeps groups moving.

> _____ *Traffic and Safety Subcommittee*
> Prepares and posts signs, sets up and maintains checkroom, keeps elevators from becoming overloaded, keeps traffic moving smoothly in tours, provides security at selected tour points, enforces fire regulations, oversees parking.

> _____ *Invitations Subcommittee*
> Compiles master invitation list, designs the printed invitation, prepares letters of invitation for special guests, determines date for mailing invitations, determines date for collecting responses, sends out invitations, monitors responses.

> _____ *Refreshments Subcommittee*
> Purchases food and paper goods, sets up buffets and beverages, helps serve guests.

_____ Organize workers to serve on above committees.

_____ Hold a joint meeting of Planning Committee and subcommittees to explain Open House plan and its purpose.

_____ Formulate a publicity plan, including deadlines for media to be contacted.

_____ Prepare copy for printed program and website, including information about tour itinerary, brief facts about the library, names of its governing board, and names of the event's Planning Committee.

_____ Hold a "day before the event" briefing meeting. Distribute event schedule to each committee member, discuss what each person will be expected to do that day, and distribute identification badges.

_____ During Open House, set up several registration tables and stagger tour schedules to avoid bottlenecks. Distribute event program as guests arrive, so that they know what to expect.

_____ After the Open House:

> _____ Mail printed program, together with appropriate letter and enclosure, to selected people who did not attend the event.

> _____ Send photos to media, and to people pictured, thanking them for their participation.

> _____ Place information about the event on the library's website.
> _____ Thank everyone who helped make the event successful.

> _____ Evaluate the Open House to determine how the next one could be improved.

A library's mission and performance in a community are valuable investment opportunities for some businesses. These investments may come in the form of sponsorships, especially when affiliation with a library event or service can be used to further a corporation's marketing strategy or corporate goals.

When matched correctly, a sponsorship is a win-win situation where a library is provided with funding or other tangible support and a business attracts new customers because its corporate objectives (e.g., developing a trusting relationship with consumers, improving its corporate image, increasing sales) have been linked with a public good.

Corporate sponsorship is an avenue of funding that many library foundations have long utilized to augment their fundraising campaigns. Big dollars can often bring big names to an event. For example, a library might attract a noted author who speaks and sells a new book, or a guest list studded with the movers and shakers prominent in a library's community might attract many potential donors for library projects. Thousands of companies invest in some form of event sponsorship because this type of investment provides an alternative to the cluttered mass media.

IT'S A MATTER OF FIT

Even small libraries and libraries new to public relations and fundraising can benefit from sponsorship opportunities. A good way to identify a business sponsor is to find businesses (of any size) that are dependent on new and repeat customers. For example, a library might design a summer reading program for children and adults that utilizes award coupons from local businesses (e.g., restaurants, bookstores, movie theaters, grocers). As library readers are introduced or reintroduced to local businesses, these retail outlets benefit. Other factors to consider when recruiting a sponsor include image compatibility, audience composition, publicity opportunities, bottom-line tie-ins, exclusivity, and value-added benefits.

DEVELOPING THE PARTNERSHIP

As in any good relationship, each party needs to make a comparable effort. But many companies don't understand the capabilities, needs, or creative marketing opportunities that nonprofit organizations can bring to a partnership. In order for a mutually beneficial exchange to exist, nonprofits must have an understanding of partnership "rules of courtship." Some common rules apply:

- The library must know what it needs.
- First impressions are everything.
- Don't enter a relationship hoping to change the corporate partner.
- One partner will always want to get serious sooner than the other.
- One-night stands are to be avoided.

"Seeking a sponsor is really about seeking a partner with whom your organization will share benefits and values, rather than simply taking them as in a donor relationship. Still, as with any relationship, entering into a partnership between a nonprofit organization and a corporation requires patience, trust, clarity, and creativity," says Kimberley Rudd, national director of marketing and development at KaBOOM!, a national nonprofit organization that fosters networks to build much-needed, safe, and accessible playgrounds.[1]

"At KaBOOM!, we try our best to 'date' our business partners rather than rush into any activity," Rudd continues. "This sets the stage for trust and clarity of goals. We want to understand their business and their goals: What is it that they hope to accomplish by aligning with our nonprofit brand? What attributes of their brand mesh with our brand, and which are different and add new value? Also, we want to be sure that the partner recognizes our mission-driven work and our goals. Toward that, we invite new partners to witness the building of a playground or the energy of a community-building training conference. For a business leader, hearing us talk about what we do is never as impactful as seeing it up close.

"We have also learned not to muddy clarity with fancy titles for sponsorship levels; it's just not us. We try to make it as clear as possible what that corporate partner's funding will provide for, and how the funding and partnership impact our mission. Finally, we push ourselves and our partners to be creative: money is important, but it's not everything and very often, our best corporate partners are those that contribute a variety of resources to us. If KaBOOM! is able to follow this courtship ritual—and we sometimes meet with forks in the road—then we believe that we are on our way to a great relationship with a corporate partner."

How does Rudd's experience at KaBOOM! translate into action for a library? The KaBOOM! model of securing corporate support (www.kaboom.org) demonstrates that "a library could identify companies that show a healthy respect for words and images and all that goes with enjoying them—companies that produce paper and microfilm, electronic books and cozy furniture, paints and snack foods," Rudd says. "Then, after researching the missions and personalities of these companies, libraries must get their attention and take them on 'dates.' Bring them into your libraries and let them see the impact reading has on your communities. Drop them notes with interesting statistics and news. Share with them trends in reading, 'hot' books for children, or new programs for serving people with disabilities. Keep them in the loop on libraries and stay on their radar screen—without being annoying, of course. Then, when you're ready to make an 'ask' of the company, know the value of what you're offering and clearly articulate the shared benefits of your partnership."

Sponsorship/event marketing is a business deal. The company that a library works with views sponsorship as a way to build its brand image, create loyal customers, and ultimately improve sales—all business propositions. So it is critical that library event planners also view this marketing opportunity as a business negotiation where organizational needs must be satisfied. Don't confuse this opportunity with a philanthropic gift. Don't beg or be shy about stating what you need. Be prepared to walk away if the deal isn't right for you, or if it is not the right time to proceed.

A CASE STUDY:
IF AT FIRST YOU DON'T SUCCEED

Just as with fundraising efforts, event planners seeking corporate partnerships should be prepared to be surprised, and should be able to be flexible with potential sponsors who suggest a modification to an event plan. Such was the case when the "A" Library approached a major corporation to request sponsorship for "A" Library's "Kids Who Read Succeed" summer reading program event.

Because of an increasing number of children participating in "A" Library's summer reading program, funds to repeat the prize giveaway of a paperback book to kids who accomplished their summer reading goals were not available. Realizing that this incentive was very popular with both children and their parents, and that it was consistent with "A" Library's mission to promote the joy of reading, the Library Board established the goal of raising $10,000 to fund the paperback give-aways for the summer reading program's special event.

When the initial ask to the corporation was denied, there was also an upside. "A" Library was told its proposal was actually better suited to the corporation's foundation, which had the stated goal of reaching and influencing elementary schoolchildren in their corporate community. The corporate executive explained how "A" Library could restructure its proposal and increase the size of its funding request. "A" Library was granted $3,000 more than its initial $5,000 request because the corporation's foundation was interested in the target audience that "A" Library could deliver. The corporation was also approached during the time in its corporate fiscal year when adequate funding was available.

STEP FIVE
Consider Logistics

There is no infallible formula for carrying out an event. With many activities often going on simultaneously, there are many details to be checked, and many chances for little things to go awry. Major areas to consider for a smoothly coordinated event include:

> The space or spaces for the event must be appropriately large or small and should be well designed to accommodate all of the event's special needs. Obstacles that detract from the event's objectives should be minimized.

> The location should provide adequate utility support (electricity, gas, water, lighting, telephones), as well as adequate numbers of computers, and photocopiers.

> Setup for the event should include consideration of tables, chairs, tents, portable toilets, security, first aid, information kiosks, sound (including sound enhancers for hearing-impaired individuals), interpreters for the deaf, lights, signage, garbage, and cleanup.

> Public service sectors must be made aware of the special event. These groups include, but are not limited to, police, fire, emergency medical services, and public works departments.

> All participants involved in the event's execution must know the event schedule and setup, their duties, and emergency procedures. Be sure to ask, "Who else needs to know?"

> All participants must know in advance whether or not they will be paid for their services, how much, and when.

> Transportation needs must be carefully considered, with special attention paid to parking, mass transit, parking permits, accessibility for disabled individuals and special requests from disabled individuals, and transportation that might be necessary within the event facility, or between event locations.

STEP SIX
Plan the Publicity

Selecting the right publicity vehicles to promote a special event takes creativity balanced with practicality. The primary objective for special event publicity is to publicize the event. Secondary objectives must also be considered. For example, the publicity might be designed to:

- inform, educate, or entertain

- increase awareness of, or attendance at, the event

- build a base of support from a specific audience

- facilitate good community relations

It is also important to organize a list of special guests who will receive VIP invitations (e.g., trustees; mayor; donors; city and governing officials; business, civic, professional, and education leaders; media) and to develop a plan for welcoming, seating, and photographing special guests.

Depending on the objectives for the publicity, librarians will want to choose from the various publicity options that are discussed in the other chapters of this book. A media plan should be developed. Here, the choices include:

- Print media (press releases and invitations, advertisements, and news coverage of event)

- Library website (photos, news article, links to other community websites)

- Television (public service announcements and news coverage of the event)

- Radio (public service announcements and talk shows)

- Direct mail (targeted to existing and potential audiences). If direct mail is used, a tracking mechanism that will allow the librarians to evaluate the usefulness of this expensive publicity mechanism should be developed.

- Specialty items (posters, flyers, bumper stickers, exhibits, billboards, balloons, envelope stuffers, refrigerator magnets, bookmarks, postage meter imprints)

STEP SEVEN
Evaluate the Event

An effective way to evaluate a special event is to evaluate each element that went into staging it—the strategies, checklist, budget, sponsors, logistics, and the effectiveness of publicity which was used. It is also most effective if these separate evaluations occur very soon after the event while details are still fresh in people's minds.

In order to solicit feedback, the event planners might want to ask guests to fill out a print or online questionnaire, or informally record comments as guests leave the event. People involved in staging the event should also be queried about the effectiveness of processes that shaped and implemented the event. A final report should be written that provides a summary of the event feedback and contains recommendations for future events.

Specific questions and observations that are used to evaluate the success of a special event should address general evaluative criteria, including:

Did the event fulfill its original objectives? If so, the evaluators might want to analyze why the event was a success in order to use it as a model for future events. If the event did not meet its objectives, evaluators should try to determine why, and develop strategies for improvement.

What elements of the event worked well and what did not? For example, were the master invitation lists appropriately targeted, or did the targeting fall short? How accurately were expenditures projected? What vendors should be used again? What items should be added to the checklist that was used?

Evaluating missed opportunities during an event is essential for avoiding potential disappointments or emergencies the next time the event is scheduled. For example, were relationships established with a company or individual that the library might partner with on some other project?

Were there missed opportunities for publicity or media coverage? For example, if the *Wall Street Journal* recently wrote an article on the subject of a library's event, and the library was the first in its region to address this subject, chances are there was a great shot at increased coverage for your event. This evaluation is the place to include a list of media outlets that could have been targeted, pointing out high-placement print and television placement possibilities that were missed.

Estimate how much time and money were spent by every person involved, from the names of every intern to key administrators. Also indicate whether these expenditures were necessary.

What factors had an impact on the event? Were these out of the library's control? What long-term solutions will help the library to maintain better control next time? Consider whether the event didn't meet its deadlines, or projected income, because of internal planning, external legal approvals, or other identifiable factors.

Given all that went into staging the event, was it worth doing?

Finally, it is very important to remember to celebrate your successes and to thank all those responsible for contributing to an event's success.

NOTE

1. Quotes from Kimberley Rudd are reprinted with permission from e-mail correspondence dated May 10, 2000.

SOURCES OF ADDITIONAL INFORMATION

Print Sources

Kotler, Philip. *Kotler on Marketing: How to Create, Win, and Dominate Markets.* New York: Free Press, 1999.

Kotler, Philip, and Alan Andreason. *Strategic Marketing for Nonprofit Organizations.* 5th ed. Upper Saddle River, N.J.: Prentice-Hall, 1996.

Shimp, Terence A. *Advertising, Promotion and Supplemental Aspects of Integrated Marketing Communications.* 4th ed. Fort Worth, Tex.: Harcourt Brace, 1997.

Webography

www.iabc.com—International Association of Business Communicators. This organization is a "knowledge network" for professionals working in the field of strategic business communications management. Through publications and research, it provides advice and instruction on effective communication strategies.

www.litlamp.com/—LitLamp. This is an online provider of communications programs for campaigns such as school-based promotions, sponsorship programs, employers and volunteers programs, event management, media campaigns, and other public relations activities. Event planners can browse sponsorship opportunities that detail tangible, commercial benefits.

www.prsa.org/ppc—Professional Practice Center Online. This online clearinghouse provides information on public relations and public relations campaigns.

www.urbanlibraries.org—Urban Libraries Council. This association of public libraries and corporations in metropolitan areas works to establish collaborations between libraries and corporations.

Desktop Publishing and Image

ANN HAMILTON

DESKTOP SOFTWARE

An "off the shelf" word-processing or desktop-publishing program is a necessity for creating public relations materials. Additionally, access to a scanner allows desktop publishers to use graphics created from the library's own print or digital photographs or from non-copyrighted sources.

A number of books and manuals are available to show users how to get the most out of a word processing package. Library "publishers" should find one they like and keep it handy. It is also very helpful to take advantage of classes covering specific word processing packages. Short, inexpensive classes and workshops are often offered by libraries, local schools, computer retailers, university continuing-education divisions, and other local educational institutions. But don't get too comfortable with the packages that are currently in use at the library. Always be on the lookout for good examples of public relations materials and ask the creators what software package was used to create them. Although it takes time and money, it is important to engage in professional development as one learns new software that may have more sophisticated features or might be better suited to the library's publication needs. Software reviews and evaluations can be found in print and on the World Wide Web through sources such as *PC Magazine*.

After learning the basics of a software package, it is possible to:

Create variety by using different fonts, type sizes, and colors. Some printers also allow changes in appearance. The font choices vary according to the printer used. However, it is important to use these features carefully. Figure 8.1 shows how poor choices can be disastrous.

Create interest by inserting topical or humorous graphics. Most word-processing software programs include graphics, and there are a number of relatively inexpensive or even free graphics programs available that can be used with them. Figure 8.2 shows how a simple graphic can form the cover or backdrop for a library publication.

FIGURE 8.1
Dangers of Inappropriately Mixing Fonts and Type Sizes

Mixing

SEVERAL

print *styles*

can obscure

your message

Example created using WordPerfect 9 and the font, size, and appearance choices available for a Hewlett-Packard DeskJet 680C printer.

FIGURE 8.2
Create Interest with Graphics

A humorous graphic can be used as a backdrop for a publication.

Create standard forms for schedules, holdings locations, and similar signs. Forms can be stored and easily revised as information changes. Figure 8.3 is a library form that was designed to provide basic information on citation style.

FIGURE 8.3
Library Form on Bibliographic Citation

How to Prepare Bibliographic Citations
for World Wide Web Pages (WWW): Turabian

For more information on Turabian Style, see: Turabian, Kate L. **A Manual for Writers of Term Papers, Theses, and Dissertations.** 6th ed., rev. by John Grossman and Alice Bennett. Chicago: University of Chicago Press, 1996.

Citations of electronic documents follow the same basic form as for print documents. The same information is needed: author, title of document, name and description of source cited, format of the item, publication information, pathway to access the item (e.g., web address) and date of your own access to the item. Materials originally issued in print should include the same information as you would for the print version, adding the information needed to locate the electronic version.

State or regional database such as GALILEO:

Note

Hiroshi Fujita, "UN Reform and Japan's Permanent Security Council Seat," **Japan Quarterly** 42 (October 1995): 436. [journal online]; available from **GALILEO: Periodical Abstracts Research;** Internet; accessed 29 September 1997.

Bibliography

Fujita, Hiroshi. "UN Reform and Japan's Permanent Security Council Seat." **Japan Quarterly** 42 (October 1995): 436–442. [journal online]; available from **GALILEO: Periodical Abstracts Research;** Internet; accessed 29 September 1997.

Note

Angelo, Bonnie. "Family and faith fire the spirit of camp meetings. church camps." **Smithsonian** 27, no. 5 (1996): 66; available from **GALILEO: Lexis/Nexis Academic Universe**; Form: General News Topics. Source: All magazines; Internet; accessed 30 October 1998.

Bibliography

Angelo, Bonnie. "Family and faith fire the spirit of camp meetings. church camps." **Smithsonian** 27, no. 5 (1996): 66; available from **GALILEO: Lexis/Nexis Academic Universe;** Form: General News Topics. Source: All magazines; Internet; accessed 30 October 1998.

Other web pages:

Note

United States, Department of Defense, "Operation Joint Endeavor Fact Sheet, 006–B: Multinational IFOR Coalition Participation," BosniaLink; available from http://www.dtic.dla.mil/bosnia/fs/fs0006b.html; Internet; accessed December 11, 1995.

United States, Department of Defense. "Operation Joint Endeavor Fact Sheet, 006–B: Multinational IFOR Coalition Participation." BosniaLink; available from http://www.dtic.dla.mil/bosnia/fs/fs006b.html; Internet; accessed December 11, 1995.

Create folded brochures. Folded brochures are created by setting the paper size to 11" × 8-1/2" (landscape) and using columns. A tri-fold brochure copy can be printed on both sides of the page with three columns of information per side. A single-fold brochure can be created using the same technique to create two columns for each side of the paper. Pictures can be added to make brochures even more attractive. Figure 8.4 is a brochure that provides information on library services available for disabled patrons.

FIGURE 8.4
Folded Brochure

LIBRARY INFORMATION FOR PERSONS WITH DISABILITIES

Zach S. Henderson Library
Georgia Southern University
May 4, 2000

Brochure 10

FOLD

PANEL 4

PANEL 1

BUILDING ACCESS

There are two main points of access to the Library. An entrance on the first floor through the Microcomputer Applications Area (MAA) is available during all hours the Library is open. The door remains locked for security purposes, but a bell by the door can be used to notify Library personnel of an individual's need for access.

Persons not wishing to enter the Library through the first floor may enter the building via ramps at the back of the building. Those access points are closest to the two parking spaces for persons with disabilities next to the Library. Anyone needing assistance in getting into the Library via the second floor may ring a bell that is located to the right of the entrance doors.

COMPUTER AND PRINT ACCESS

The equipment and software used to provide access to the Library's online and print materials is housed in the MAA on the first floor so that it is available during all hours the Library is open.

The Library has the following equipment available in the MAA:

- A closed-circuit television (CCTV) device for magnifying written materials that can be used for any printed matter, including bound periodicals. It does not have a color monitor, but it does provide contrast controls to assist varying levels of viewing.

- A computer with a large screen monitor that has software that permits "hands-off" control of the computer, software that will read aloud any material scanned or otherwise brought up on screen, and software that permits a scanned page to be converted to word processor text instead of picture format.

- A scanner for scanning materials into the computer so that they may be read aloud or used with other computer programs.

All tables used on the first floor meet the height requirements specified by the ADA.

Assistance in learning to use this equipment is available in the MAA Monday through Friday from 8:00 A.M. until 5:00 P.M.

MICROFORM ACCESS

There is a special lens available for microform reader/printers designed to magnify the reader screen so that persons with limited vision should be able to read enough of an article to know whether they want to make a copy. The lens is available through the Access Services Department on the second floor.

MATERIALS ACCESS

Persons who are unable to retrieve books and other materials from Library shelves may get assistance at the Circulation Desk on the second floor. The staff at the Circulation Desk

FOLD

PANEL 2

will also be able to provide access to the staff elevator if the public elevator is out of order.

TELECOMMUNICATIONS FOR THE DEAF

The Library has an Ultratec Minicom IV TDD (Telecommunications device for the Deaf) at the circulation desk on the second floor. The number for the TDD is (912) 871-1314. It is a portable version with printing option, and includes a bright, 20-character display tilted to increase viewing comfort, and a 4-row keyboard specially designed for easy typing. An 8000-character memory allows messages to be saved, and a built-in voice announces that an outgoing call is being made by TDD. TDD access is available during all Library hours.

EMERGENCY PREPAREDNESS

The Library has recently installed an updated emergency alarm system that features alarm notifications by recorded voice messages, siren sounds, and flashing strobe lights. If the alarm system is activated for any reason, all people in the Library at the time are to leave the building immediately in a calm, orderly manner.

The Library has a detailed emergency plan in place to assist users during evacuations of the building. During an emergency, Library employees are assigned to check all areas of the Library for persons with disabilities.

Elevators should not be used in most emergencies. Persons on the first and second floors have access to building exits without the use of elevators. Persons on the third or fourth floors who cannot move to other floors without the use of an elevator should assemble in front of the public elevator. Library personnel are assigned to check those assembly points and escort individuals to the nearest safe stairwell where they can wait for properly trained emergency personnel to give them assistance in moving to the lower floors. Radios are available for maintaining communication from the stairwells.

SUGGESTIONS AND COMMENTS

Suggestions and comments concerning the Library's services for persons with disabilities are welcome at any time. Suggestions are reviewed by the Library's administration daily and are used to correct immediate deficiencies and to plan for the implementation of new services. We are especially interested in evaluative information concerning the hardware and computer software we have installed to maximize access for persons with disabilities, and would welcome the opportunity to meet with anyone who would like to assist us with the specifications for such equipment.

Zach S. Henderson Library
Post Office Box 8074
Georgia Southern University
Statesboro, Georgia 30460-8074
Telephone: (912) 681-5115
Schedule Information: (912) 681-5028
Homepage:<http://www2.gasou.edu/library>

PANEL 3

PHOTOCOPIERS

Brochures, flyers, posters, and other public relations materials can be reproduced easily on a photocopier. It is usually cheaper to use a photocopier than to have materials professionally printed. It is especially helpful if the photocopy machine can be used to enlarge or reduce copy. If that feature is available, the ability to cut and paste information and graphics to create attractive pieces is almost unlimited.

Some helpful hints to keep in mind:

Use correcting fluid sparingly and with precision in order to keep the master copy and additional copies clean and professional looking.

When the sheet being copied does not reach all areas of the copier plate, place another larger piece of paper behind that sheet to prevent lines from appearing on final copy.

Enhance creative possibilities for a photocopy machine by maintaining a supply of paper in a variety of colors, textures, finishes, and weights. Use color to increase the effectiveness of the piece. To attract attention, use a bright neon color. For a more subtle message, use a pastel.

Keep at least a small supply of every size paper your photocopy machine will accept. The more choices available, the more flexibility for tailoring public relations materials to specific needs.

COLOR PRINTERS AND COLOR COPIERS

Color printers are much less expensive than in the past. Using a color printer for relatively small runs of documents greatly expands a library's ability to create attractive signs, announcements, and posters. Librarians located on a university campus, at a school, or as part of a city/county government should check prices at their host institution's print shop before printing large runs on library printers. Although high-quality color copiers are still quite expensive, a library or host institution that produces great quantities of promotional literature may want to consider investing in this equipment.

DIVERSITY

Library patrons and library staff are diverse. It is important to keep that diversity in mind when planning and creating public relations materials. The diversity of the target audience should be considered throughout the creative process. Some questions to ask and some things to keep in mind include:

Should the program/display/printed piece appeal to men and women (boys and girls)? If so, choose graphics and colors that will catch the attention of either. Do not place displays too high or too low to be accessible to all members of the target audience.

Should the program/display/printed piece appeal to persons of different ages? If so, keep all of the potential age groups in mind. Do not use graphics that are targeted only at a small segment of the target audience.

Should the program/display/printed piece be produced in more than one language? If patrons include persons of a number of different nationalities, materials produced in those different languages can be welcome. This is particularly true of brochures describing library services and directional signs assisting patrons in locating materials. Care should be taken, however, in the use of multiple languages. Can a program be presented in more than one language? If not, care should be taken to ensure that flyers advertising it do not imply that more than one language will be used.

Should the program/display/printed piece be accessible to persons with disabilities? Tactile displays, audio recordings, and braille copies of descriptive materials can assist persons with visual disabilities. Having a signer present during a program or providing printed texts of audio presentations can assist persons with hearing disabilities. Displays should be as accessible as possible to persons with physical disabilities. Web pages must also be accessible to individuals with visual disabilities who may be using front-end software that reads computer information to them. This may mean that for every heavily graphic web page, the library also provides a "text-only" web page that can be interpreted by "reading" software.

Librarians designing public relations should always keep in mind the multicultural version of the Golden Rule created by Judith Sessions, dean and university librarian at Miami University of Ohio: "Do unto others as they would prefer to be done unto."[1]

CONSISTENCY

Creating a consistent visual image for the library is critical. It is very important that a library have an overall policy regarding promotional materials, documents, and web pages that are produced at the library or distributed under the library's letterhead. If a policy does not exist, but the library (or its host institution) has a separate public relations department, employees in that area can be consulted concerning consistency of image. For example, a member of the public relations department for the city, county, school district, or academic institution could provide assistance with a special library public-relations project.

Consistency in terms of formats and colors for printed pieces is also important. For example, a better impression is made if signs are printed on the same color paper and placed in holders, rather than generating many signs and flyers in different colors and attaching them to every available surface. The same considerations apply to library websites. All of a library's web pages should be consistent in their design and navigation, even if the content of each web page differs. And, most importantly, web pages must be consistently updated so that the information presented is accurate.

Getting information to patrons is important, but the long-lasting effects of a poorly designed public-relations document can far outweigh urgency. Make time to think about issues of consistency in all public relations efforts.

THINGS TO AVOID

One should always be careful in library publications to avoid:

Sexism in language or graphics. It is extremely important to ensure that even subtle sexism has been avoided. In order to ensure that public relations materials are appropriate, many people should be asked to review drafts in order to solicit the perspectives of many different cultural backgrounds.

Stereotyping and racism in graphics or language. It is easy to lose an important segment of the target audience if stereotyping or racism is inadvertently included in a message. Again, as many people as possible should review drafts to ensure that subtle forms of racism or stereotyping have been avoided.

Ageism. People are active and involved well into their 80s and even 90s. Older adults should be portrayed as active in library promotional materials and, most importantly, they should be involved in the design of library promotions.

NOTE

1. Quoted with permission from a presentation by Judith Sessions entitled "Valuing Diversity" made at the 2000 SOLINET annual membership meeting.

SOURCES OF ADDITIONAL INFORMATION

Bain, Steve. *Fundamental Quark XPress 4.* Berkeley, Calif.: Osborn McGraw Hill, 1998.

Blake, Barbara Radke. *Creating Newsletters, Brochures, and Pamphlets: A How-to-Do-It Manual.* New York: Neal-Schuman, 1992.

Crawford, Walt. *Desktop Publishing for Librarians.* Boston: G. K. Hall, 1990.

Devall, Sandra Lentz, and Esther Kibby. *Desktop Publishing Style Guide.* Albany, N.Y.: Delmar, 1999.

Green, Chuck. *The Desktop Publisher's Idea Book: One-of-a-Kind Projects, Expert Tips, and Hard-to-Find Sources.* 2nd ed. New York: Random House, 1997.

Leerburger, Benedict A. *Promoting and Marketing the Library.* Boston: G. K. Hall, 1989.

Parker, Roger C. *Looking Good in Print.* 11th ed. Scottsdale, Ariz.: Coriolis Group, 2000.

Roberts, Anne F. *Public Relations for Librarians.* Englewood, Colo.: Libraries Unlimited, 1989.

Sherman, Steve. *ABC's of Library Promotion.* 3rd ed. Metuchen, N.J.: Scarecrow, 1992.

Slaughter, Scott. *Easy Digital Photography.* Grand Rapids, Mich.: Abacus, 1997.

Street, Rita, and Robert Street. *Creative Newsletters and Annual Reports.* Gloucester, Mass.: Rockport, 1998.

Walters, Suzanne. *Marketing: A How-to-Do-It Manual for Librarians.* New York: Neal-Schuman, 1992.

Wills, Scott. *Computer Tips for Artists, Designers and Desktop Publishers.* New York: W. W. Norton, 1997.

Wolfe, Lisa A. *Library Public Relations, Promotions and Communications: A How-to-Do-It Manual.* New York: Neal-Schuman, 1997.

9 Public Relations Lessons: Selected Annotated Bibliography

ANDREA L. MILLER

It's easy to complain about mayhem and fluff in the news. And it's convenient to blame journalists for not covering issues and causes—stories that might help solve the problems our society faces.

But the truth is, every citizen shares the blame with the news media. We do not offer journalists enough opportunities—in the right packaging and at the right time—to cover causes and important issues.

Nonprofit organizations and activists are certainly part of the problem. On tight budgets, they often argue that trying to get media attention distracts them from doing the real work—managing programs, organizing, fund-raising, recruiting volunteers, and so on. So they are left struggling to save the world in the dim light of obscurity and wondering why more people don't value what they do. And worse, they never benefit from all the ways that getting media coverage can make their work easier.

(Jason Salzman, *Making the News: A Guide for Nonprofits and Activists*)

One cannot deny the importance of positioning an organization and its administrators to lead. The purpose of this annotated bibliography is to provide a number of significant and practical resources for librarians and library administrators who are planning to engage in public relations. Nonprofit organizations have long ignored the political environment in which they operate, and, as Salzman indicates, libraries will never benefit from the media if they do not work with it to bring their work and their programs out of obscurity.

The selections in this annotated bibliography have been written by experts in the areas of marketing, business, communications, and advertising. These professionals have been surviving for years by exploiting partnerships with the media in order to "benefit from all the ways that getting media coverage can make their work easier." Only monographs and articles from 1991 to the present have been included in this bibliography, and all are new from the previous edition of this book. Most resources are very practical, and in some cases, the resources may be used as handbooks to guide readers as they strategically plan media events and work to garner more public relations exposure. Also new to this edition are training seminars and Internet marketing resources which were not available during the writing of the previous edition.

Although most of the resources that follow focus on the world of profit, the lessons learned from that world are extremely beneficial and can easily be adapted for nonprofit organizations. More and more is being written on the importance of nonprofit organizations building positive relationships with the media as the financial and political ramifications for their survival are recognized. Since the first edition of this book was researched and written, more publications have been written specifically for libraries of all types, and for school library media centers in particular. This trend is extremely encouraging and may be a reflection of the fact that librarians are realizing the critical importance of positioning themselves and their services and programs in the marketplace through the aggressive application of public relations techniques and marketing strategies.

SELECTED ANNOTATED BIBLIOGRAPHY

Public Relations and the Media

Alexander, David. *How You Can Manipulate the Media: Guerrilla Methods to Get Your Story Covered by TV, Radio, and Newspapers.* Boulder, Colo.: Paladin, 1993.

Librarians familiar with Paladin Press know that its publishing focus is just on the fringe of the First Amendment, so any title with the word "guerrilla" in it is probably not surprising. David Alexander, however, is not an expert in hand-to-hand combat. He is a media insider who has shared his secrets in this book on how to "spin" public relations to accomplish goals. As one would expect with any insider, Alexander is able to tell readers how to use the media for their best interests and how to position an organization to make the media want to focus on it.

Beekman, Carol T. "That Old PR Magic." *Public Relations Tactics* 5, no. 9 (September 1998): 12.

Five magic tricks are proposed for being an effective public relations officer. This article is particularly good for libraries, since advice is given for dealing with the press when the chief executive officer is out of town, when the organization is trying to publish new brochures with little money, when staff budgets are cut, and when approvals are needed expediently.

Bonk, Kathy, Henry Griggs, and Emily Tynes. *The Jossey-Bass Guide to Strategic Communications for Nonprofits: A Step-by-Step Guide to Working with the Media to: Generate Publicity, Enhance Fundraising, Build Membership, Change Public Policy, Handle Crises.* San Francisco: Jossey-Bass, 1999.

Originally published by the Communications Consortium Media Center and its founder, Kathy Bonk, this expanded edition is a workbook for all types of nonprofit groups that wish to create a clear strategic plan for advancing their agendas. Very comprehensive in scope, this toolkit for public relations includes new media and technologies as well as traditional media sources. This book guides nonprofits through the development of clear public relations objectives, design of a campaign, and media targeting within a strategic communications plan.

Boyd, Andrew. *The Activist Cookbook: Creative Actions for a Fair Economy.* Boston: United for a Fair Economy, 1997.

This atypical public relations textbook assists readers by offering creative and artistic means to energize their meetings, conferences, campaigns, and media events. Librarians will surely be excited about forming partnerships with their local artists to think more creatively about their media events.

Harness, Jan Sokoloff. "Media Relations Training: Make It Work for You." *Public Relations Tactics* (December 1999): 16.

Harness's target audience is media relations firms, but her message concerning media relations training for an organization is one that librarians should heed. Just as soon as one of the staff answers the telephone, responds to an e-mail, or greets a patron at the door, media relations has begun. The author makes suggestions for training staff on media relations so that everyone is working for the organization as a media relations person every hour of the workday.

Hunter, Glenn. "Intimidated by Media Interviewers? Here's Some Expert Advice." *Nashville Business Journal* 14, no. 48 (November 20, 1998): 50.

As the managing editor of the *Dallas Business Journal,* Hunter believes in following the example of Ken Fairchild, who teaches businesspeople how to handle reporters. Fairchild proposes preparing for interviews ahead of time through role-playing, practicing being comfortable with oneself in any situation, expecting respect, and being honest. Other suggestions include ways to handle the media in order to obtain better stories about an organization.

Kramer, John E. "Get Your Ph.D. in Media Relations." *Public Relations Tactics* (December 1999): 13–14.

Kramer's message is to "personalize, humanize, and dramatize" public relations messages. Personalizing involves matching reporters with their preferred medium and individual interests. Humanizing involves demonstrating how the particular story affects people's lives or one life in particular. Dramatizing is the ability to demonstrate the urgency of a message.

Neville, Debbie. "Creating a Press-Friendly Web Site." *Public Relations Tactics* (December 1999): 6.

In a society where people feel glutted by information, it is critical to place strategic messages about an organization on its web page. It is also important to both name and register a website to ensure that the press can readily find it, and to place the easy-to-remember website address on all of the organization's print materials. Organizational websites should be constructed so that they enable interaction and they should include a press guest book.

Ryan, Charlotte. *Prime Time Activism: Media Strategies for Grassroots Organizing.* Cambridge, Mass.: South End, 1991.

South End Press characterizes *Prime Time Activism* as a book that "fills the void" between very practical toolkit manuals and heavy tomes of media theory. This book does, however, include a good measure of analysis of the media, so one should not expect a light read. Its value lies in its ability to help readers understand the media so that they can work effectively within mass media's complex structures.

Salzman, Jason. *Making the News: A Guide for Nonprofits and Activists.* Boulder, Colo.: Westview, 1998.

Salzman's practical and easy-to-read tips for individuals who are responsible for nonprofit public relations include suggestions for developing formal media relationships, writing news releases, and giving interviews to the media. A major portion of the book is written to help the "not so media savvy" think about ways to create media coverage for their organizations with minimal labor. Readers will learn how to pitch stories to reporters, lobby editorial writers, write op-ed pieces, use a wide variety of community announcement venues, and even influence political cartoonists to include a nonprofit's causes and promotions in their work. The resource section of the book includes bibliographic references for public relations and for general reading about the media, lists of news outlets, and directories of professional fundraisers and communications consultants.

Stewart, Joan. "Tips for Breaking Bread with Reporters." *Public Relations Tactics* (December 1999): 22.

This effective checklist for getting past nervousness when meeting with reporters focuses on maintaining ongoing and open communications with reporters through lunches.

Wade, John. *Dealing Effectively with the Media: What You Need to Know about Print, Radio and Television Interviews.* Los Altos, Calif.: Crisp, 1992.

Cited in Salzman's book as an excellent resource on interviewing, this primer takes the reader step-by-step through the process of how to garner an interview, prepare for it, be successful during the interview, and follow up after it is over. The first part of the book is a basic text on understanding the media, its power, types of interviews, and their specific purposes.

Public Relations and Business

Burton, Valorie. "Personal PR Skills Are Just as Important as Business Savvy." *Dallas Business Journal* 22, no. 13 (November 20, 1998): B8.

Burton, president of a marketing communications firm in Dallas, suggests that having excellent people skills, or "personal PR," is often far more important than having excellent PR skills. Often, it is etiquette that makes the biggest impression on individuals with whom an organization is working. Returning phone calls, writing thank-you notes, and avoiding habitual complaining are all elements that will give an organization a "personal PR" edge.

Caywood, Clarke L. *The Handbook of Strategic Public Relations and Integrated Communications.* New York: McGraw-Hill, 1997.

Caywood has reached out into the worlds of journalism, communications, and business to provide studies of how 13 key industries handle the critical issues surrounding public relations in order to survive in today's marketplace.

Dilenschneider, Robert L. "Public Relations for the New Millennium: Back to Social Responsibility." *Public Relations Strategist* 5, no. 1 (spring 1999): 12–16.

The prosperity of the public relations industry at the end of the 20th century will have a reversal of fortune at the start of the 21st century. The author compares the changes in communications and worldwide government over a 20-year period to highlight the fact that two decades can cause huge changes in business and government. In response to these changes, businesses should expect public relations firms to have made the Internet and other cutting-edge technologies critical components of their expertise. The author further reflects on critical trends in the new environment, some of which may encourage businesses to negate the public interest. Since the public has been growing more and more discontented with business and the economy, the author strongly suggests that business and public relations return to addressing social ills through social responsibility.

Hadaway, Terry. "News Interviews: They Don't Have to Be Like Root Canals." *Atlanta Business Chronicle* 21, no. 14 (September 11, 1998): 60A.

Advice on how to get fair media coverage for an organization and its events includes avoiding an organization's tendency to self-sabotage its media relationships and other media opportunities.

Ihator, Augustine S. "Effective Public Relations Techniques for the Small Business in a Competitive Market Environment." *Public Relations Quarterly* 43, no. 2 (summer 1998): 28–32.

Organizations that wish to remain competitive in today's market economy must recognize the importance of effective public relations. They must also maintain relationships with the media, stay involved in community affairs, and utilize online and traditional print media resources.

Levine, Michael. *Guerrilla P.R.: How You Can Wage an Effective Publicity Campaign . . . without Going Broke.* New York: Harper, 1994.

One of Hollywood's most successful publicists reveals his secrets on how to obtain PR for a business or for other types of ventures. Libraries will find his suggestions especially useful, since the focus is on public relations without high costs. All facets of PR are covered, including press releases, interviewing, and creating media events. Levine's perspective is that getting a great deal of media attention is not really the point. Instead, it is all about the quality of the messages that are sent to the media.

Levinson, Jay Conrad. *Guerrilla Marketing: Secrets for Making Big Profits from Your Small Business.* 3rd ed. Chicago: Houghton Mifflin, 1998.

A completely revised and expanded edition of his now-classic title that began the guerrilla revolution, Levinson moves his "take-no-prisoners" approach to marketing into the 21st century with strategies for marketing on the Internet and for using other cutting-edge technologies. With new businesses and start-up companies appearing in ever-growing numbers, their leaders as well as those of other small organizations will find this new edition to be invaluable. Libraries who want to be included with other fast-growing markets will want to keep this handbook nearby for frequent consultation.

_____. *Mastering Guerrilla Marketing: 100 Profit-Producing Insights that You Can Take to the Bank.* Chicago: Houghton Mifflin, 1999.

Though obviously not intended for a nonprofit audience, this book is still useful for its advice regarding styles and attitudes that are critical in marketing. Levinson takes 11 critical areas—planning, weaponry, media, online, direct response, people, attitudes, technology, economizing, creativity, and action—and presents a simple approach to marketing in today's technologically focused marketplace. As with all of the *Guerrilla* titles, the author demands action from his readers in his strongly motivational approach to the subject.

Levinson, Jay Conrad, and Seth Godin. *The Guerrilla Marketing Handbook.* Chicago: Houghton Mifflin, 1995.

This handbook, with its money-back guarantee, provides chapters that focus on different advertising methods and ways to keep the costs of advertising low.

Levinson, Jay Conrad, and Charles Rubin. *Guerrilla Advertising: Cost-Effective Techniques for Small-Business Success.* Chicago: Houghton Mifflin, 1994.

Well known for his guerrilla approach to marketing and advertising both in his book series and in his speaking engagements, Levinson teaches readers how advertising works and how to get the most benefit from every dollar spent. The author shares both his successes and failures in advertising so that readers can learn from them and profit.

Morris, Kelly. "Honesty, Preparation Can Help You Survive a Media Interview." *San Antonio Business Journal* 12, no. 26 (August 7, 1998): 18.

As vice president and director of public relations for the Atkins Agency, Morris offers pointed advice about giving interviews to the media. Interviewees are challenged to remember that an interview will either help or hurt the organization, and that it is up to the individual giving the interview to determine whether or not it will go well and whether there will be regrets when it appears in print. Successful strategies are presented, as are strategies that should *never* be used.

Ogden, James R. *Developing a Creative and Innovative Integrated Marketing Communication Plan: A Working Model.* New York: Prentice Hall, 1998.

Ogden suggests ways to develop a marketing plan and to manage the marketing component of a business. The textbook has a greater focus on the management of marketing than on building relationships with the media. However, the ideas are easily transferred to libraries and the more global perspective that includes media relations is helpful for those interested in the bigger picture.

Yale, David. *The Publicity Handbook: How to Maximize Publicity for Products, Services, and Organizations.* Lincolnwood, Ill.: NCT/Contemporary, 1991.

This comprehensive handbook takes an organization through the step-by-step process of developing a publicity plan. Especially useful is the extensive list of sources and services that are available to publicists so that *anyone* attempting to launch a successful campaign can compete with the professional media manipulators.

Public Relations and Communications

Yadin, Daniel L. *Creative Marketing Communications: A Guide to Planning, Skills and Techniques.* 2nd ed. London: Kogan Page, 1998.

Yadin's practical approach to communications techniques and skills will be useful for individuals who wish to improve their writing skills and apply them in all areas of media. The glossary/reference guide at the end of the book does have a British flavor, which may not meet everyone's needs in the United States.

Public Relations for Libraries

Blake, Barbara Radke, and Barbara L. Stein. *Creating Newsletters, Brochures, and Pamphlets: A How-to-Do-It Manual for School and Public Librarians.* New York: Neal-Schuman, 1992.

This edition does not include information on the use of technology and Internet sites for writing assistance. However, it is still valuable for its timeless advice on writing well, planning and budgeting for publications, understanding desktop publishing and the basic principles of graphic design, and managing the paperwork associated with bulk mail.

Flowers, Helen F. *Public Relations for School Library Media Programs: 500 Ways to Influence People and Win Friends for Your School Library Media Center.* New York: Neal-Schuman, 1998.

Flowers coaches school media specialists to understand that public relations is part of everything that they are and do. Additionally, since PR is very dependent upon the person who manages it, she exhorts those involved in public relations to present themselves professionally and appropriately. She then proceeds to a chapter-by-chapter approach to assist media specialists in building influence with all of their constituents, beginning with students and including staff, administrators, parents, community members, and legislators. This book is an excellent companion to Gary Hartzell's *Building Influence for the School Librarian.*

Hartzell, Gary N. *Building Influence for the School Librarian.* Worthington, Ohio: Linworth, 1994.

Hartzell provides advice from a former principal's perspective. He believes that if school library media specialists build relationships with individuals and groups who are important to a dynamic media center program, these individuals and groups will help library media specialists to "grow" their programs. In what should be required reading for all school library media specialists, Hartzell points out that if individuals in a school community do not realize the value of school library media centers, they will not support them.

Johnson, Doug. *The Indispensable Librarian: Surviving (and Thriving) in School Media Centers.* Worthington, Ohio: Linworth, 1997.

While the entirety of this book does not focus on public relations, one chapter does provide school media specialists with a guide to assist critical players in understanding "what's in it for me/them," or "WIIFM." This chapter will help librarians explain, to school administrators, a school library media center's needs for significant funding and staffing.

Walters, Suzanne. *Marketing: A How-to-Do-It Manual for Librarians.* New York: Neal-Schuman, 1992.

Walters takes the librarian through the marketing planning process to identify product, pricing, placement, and promotion as these relate to libraries and their programs and services. A sample plan is included, and, as with all of the How-to-Do-It series titles, the author provides very practical advice supplemented with many graphics for comprehension.

Wolfe, Lisa A. *Library Public Relations, Promotions, and Communications: A How-to-Do-It Manual.* New York: Neal-Schuman, 1997.

In addition to its coverage of traditional public relations techniques, this guide also provides valuable information on how to create a corporate identity for the library; utilize new technologies; launch successful media campaigns; and keep the library in the forefront of the community. A very complete appendix provides samples of communications and a variety of useful resources.

Webography

Public Relations Society of America. *PR Links.*
http://www.prsa.org/ppc/prlink.html.

The Professional Practice Center of the PRSA provides links to over 40 Internet sites that serve as gateways to public relations information. All links are continuously updated to maintain their accuracy and to add new resources. Librarians should bookmark this site for themselves and their patrons.

Roman, Anna M. *Public Relations Resources.*
http://www.geocities.com/wallstreet/2448/welcome.htm.

This listing of useful public relations Internet sites also includes easy-to-read articles and advice.

Traynor Kitching & Associates. *Marketing Magic.*
http://www.tka.co.uk/magic/home.htm.

Intended for the business sector, this site provides marketing tips, articles, and links to other sites whose focus is on the use of traditional media and online resources to become more profitable. An online collection of recommended business titles is provided, as well as a link to Amazon.com.

Ventures Online. *Internet Marketing Info and Resources.*
http://www.venturesonline.com/internet_marketing.html.

This website provides marketing tips and tools to increase a business's or organization's profile through online marketing. One of the services provided is "reciprocal linking"—Ventures Online will place links to organizations on their website if the organizations will place links to Ventures Online at their local websites.

Training and Consulting

Cypress Media Group.
http://www.cypressmedia.net.
E-mail address: cypressmedia@mindspring.com.

With over 20 years of experience in advertising, public relations, and training, Cypress Media Group will offer on-site training sessions to five or more individuals in an organization or will provide consultation by phone, fax, e-mail, or Internet. Initial consultations and needs assessments are at no charge. The group's public relations experience includes crisis and emergency PR, image consulting, government relations, proposal writing, and consulting. Its employees offer training seminars in all areas of media skills and public relations, including writing, speaking, media and public relations, problem solving, active listening, and time management.

CONTRIBUTORS

Paula Banks is community relations coordinator of the Medina (Ohio) County District Library system. She is responsible for all aspects of public relations for the system, including producing news releases, creating and editing five different Medina County District Library newsletters, and developing marketing campaigns and displays. She has served as chair of the Library Administration and Management Association (LAMA) of the American Library Association (Public Relations Section) and is active in Ohio Library Council community relations activities. She has worked in library public relations for 11 years.

Katharina J. Blackstead is library advancement officer at the University Libraries of Notre Dame. She has published on academic library history, development, and marketing, is an active participant in DORAL (Development Officers of Research and Academic Libraries), and has chaired committees and discussion groups within the Association of College and Research Libraries (ACRL) and LAMA of the American Library Association. She currently chairs the Public Relations Section of LAMA.

William Buchanan is associate professor of library science at Clarion University of Pennsylvania. Prior to joining the Clarion faculty, he worked as both a public and academic librarian. Before coming to librarianship, Buchanan worked as the director of public information for a large nonprofit agency, and he has also worked as a newspaper reporter, feature writer, and editor.

Dorothy Christiansen is head of the M. E. Grenander Department of Special Collections and Archives, University Libraries, University at Albany, State University of New York (SUNY). She serves as editor of the SUNY Libraries' newsletter, *Library Update*. In 1997 she was co-curator of the exhibit "Once upon a Drawing: The Picture Book Illustrations of Marcia Brown" and organized the companion conference on "Once upon a Time: Folklore and Fairy Tales in Children's Literature." She has chaired the SUNY Libraries' Exhibits Committee and has ongoing involvement in the Libraries' public relations and exhibits programs.

Ann Hamilton is associate university librarian at Georgia Southern University (Statesboro). Her duties include coordination of building renovation and maintenance for the Zach S. Henderson Library, which offers access to more than 300 computers during its 24-hour service schedule. Hamilton supervises the systems department that provides computer hardware and software support for the library, and coordinates automated systems implementation. She is immediate past president of the Georgia Library Association, and has been active in the ALA and the Southeastern Library Association for a number of years.

Susan M. Hilton is assistant professor in the Department of Communication at Clarion University of Pennsylvania. Her teaching is focused on print and electronic design for mass media and instructional design functions. Her research and production areas focus on interactive multimedia.

Chandler Jackson is director of the Library at the University of Great Falls in Great Falls, Montana. He has been active in the LAMA Public Relations Section and currently chairs its Publications Committee. He is also the chair-elect of the LAMA Fund Raising and Financial Development Section and has served as chair of the Public Relations in Academic Libraries Discussion Group of the ACRL.

Rashelle S. Karp is associate vice president for academic affairs at Clarion University of Pennsylvania. She is an active editor of books and journal articles and has published extensively in areas of interest to public and academic librarians. Karp was professor of library science in the Department of Library Science at Clarion University for 13 years, and served as interim dean of libraries at the university for four years.

Patricia J. Marini is associate professor of communication at Clarion University of Pennsylvania. Her areas of research and expertise include graphic design and instructional design of digital materials for print media. She is a principal partner in Legacy Learning Systems, which provides the design of data reports for various federal agencies and Fortune 500 companies.

Debora Meskauskas is public information officer of the Arlington Heights Memorial Library (Illinois), and is responsible for planning and budgeting the library's public information program directed at the 75,000 tax-supporting residents of Arlington Heights. The library's Public Information Office manages all library publications and graphics, and acts as spokesperson in representing the library to print and broadcast media. Meskauskas has worked as a public relations practitioner in hospitals and in public relations firms in Chicago, Cleveland, and Florida.

Andrea L. Miller is associate professor of library science at Clarion University of Pennsylvania. She is a member of the *School Library Media Research* Editorial Board Committee (American Association of School Librarians) and is the coeditor of its online dissertation column. Additionally, she is the cofounder and director of the Institute for the Study and Development of School Library Information Centers, and she writes and presents on topics that include collaboration, copyright, information literacy, technology in the K–12 environment, and building influence for libraries. Miller's teaching areas include library management, non-book resources, children's literature, storytelling, and teaching methods.

Lori M. Norris is head of circulation at Clarion University of Pennsylvania. Her professional interests and expertise are in the areas of library public relations, customer service, management information systems, and supervision of student assistants.

Eric C. Shoaf is head of the Preservation Department at Brown University Library, with administrative responsibility for the Bindery, Repair Unit, Conservation Lab, NEH Preservation Unit, Collection Storage and Care Unit, preservation planning, staff and user education programs, and reformatting and digital preservation projects. He also oversees the library off-site storage program.

Mary S. Wilson is instructor in the Department of Communication at Clarion University of Pennsylvania. Her professional interests and expertise are in the areas of newswriting, message design, and public relations. Her research focuses on niche publications for disabled individuals. Prior to coming to Clarion, Wilson was involved in community and public relations for the U.S. Navy.

INDEX